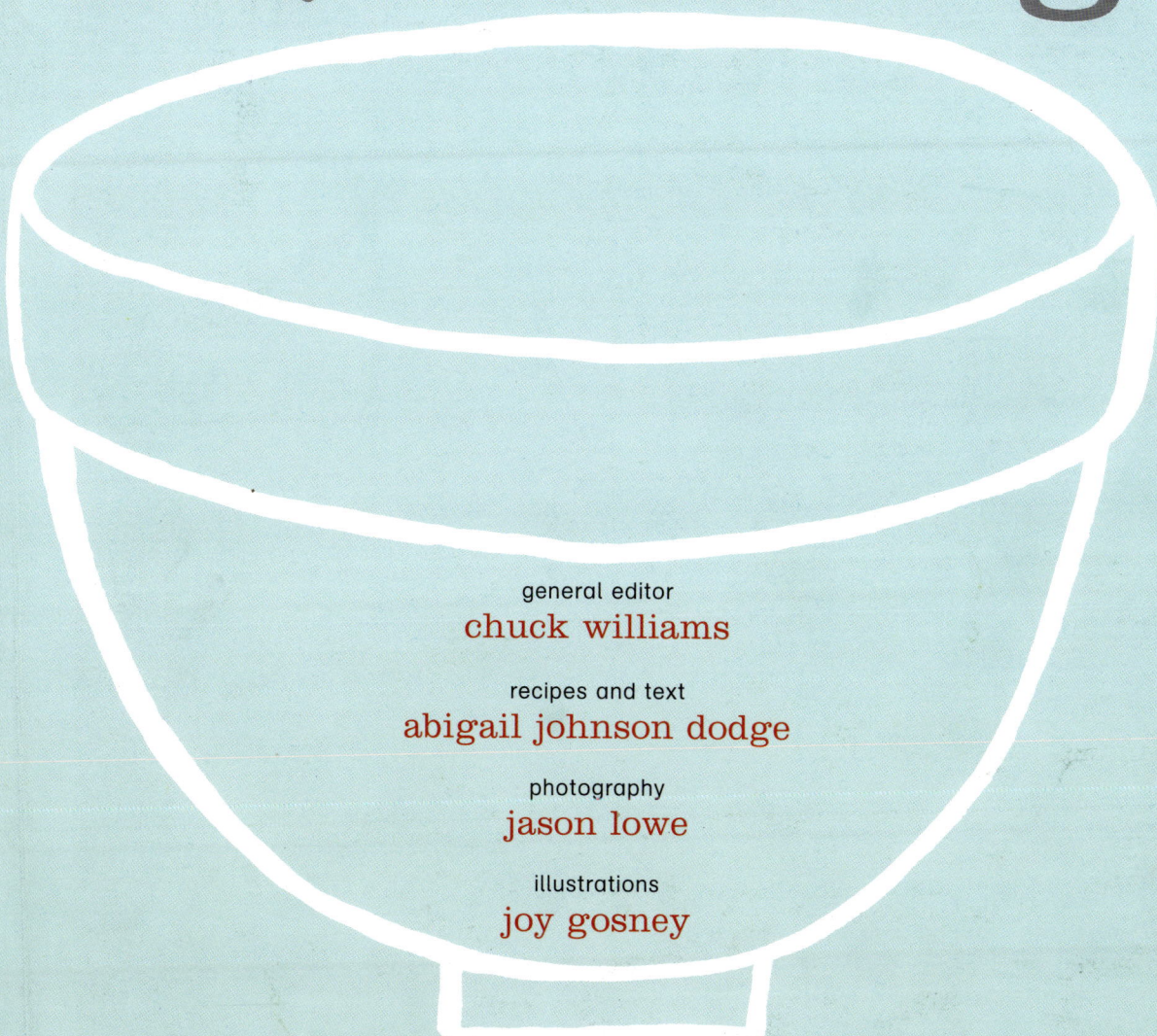

kids baking

general editor
chuck williams

recipes and text
abigail johnson dodge

photography
jason lowe

illustrations
joy gosney

INDEX

contents

mmmmm! what will you choose to bake today?

cookies

cakes & cupcakes

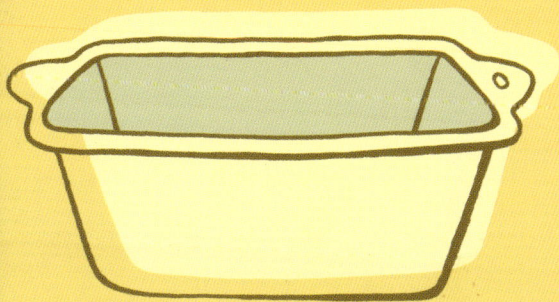

yeast breads

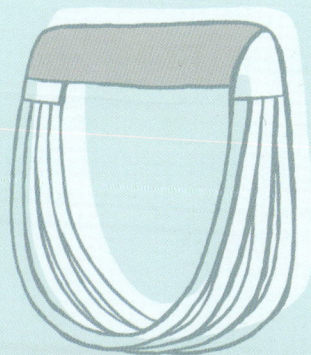

glossary

While many cookbooks have been written for kids, few, if any, are specifically about baking. Many adults find baking intimidating, and with our busy lives and the availability of baked goods at supermarkets, most children are not exposed to the fun of baking the way they once were, at their parents' sides.

This is why a book like this one is so important. It teaches kids the basics every good baker should know. Even better, it features recipes that the whole family will enjoy making and eating, so parents can bake from the book right alongside their children.

Each easy-to-read recipe includes step-by-step photographs that will help kids understand the recipes better. There are also detailed descriptions of baking techniques, pictures of the necessary tools, and a glossary of common baking terms. Finally, the recipes range from easy to more challenging, making this a book that can be enjoyed by every kid, from those who just want to bake cookies, to those who want to learn about baking breads, pies, and cakes.

Chuck Williams

hey kids!

Always ask an adult for help and be extra cautious when using sharp knives and electric mixers and handling hot baking sheets and pans. If you are new to baking, look for the "easy!" recipes to start.

hey parents!

The recipes in this cookbook are intended for kids, age 6 and up, to use with as much independence as possible. However, all cooking and baking require certain precautions. Only you can gauge how much support you will need to give to your children as they work through these recipes. You can help your children by reviewing the recipe with them before they begin and identifying any steps that may require more adult supervision. Enjoy the process, and the outcome will be equally delicious!

basics

Legend has it that whoever
eats the last piece of bread
has to kiss the cook!

playing it safe

- Always ask an adult for help when you have questions.
- Be careful with sharp knives and tools.
- Wash your hands with warm water and soap before you touch any food.
- Tie back long hair to keep it out of your way.
- Roll up your sleeves and wear an apron to keep your clothes clean while you bake.
- Clear off and clean a space big enough to work comfortably.
- Rinse and dry fruits and vegetables before you use them.
- Stay in the kitchen while the stove or oven is on.
- Use dry oven mitts to handle hot pans. Wet oven mitts will burn you.
- Let pans cool before putting them in the sink or cleaning them up.
- Clean up spills, tools, and work surfaces as you go.

how to follow a recipe

- Before you start, carefully read the entire recipe.
- Make sure you have enough time to complete the recipe without rushing.
- Gather all the tools and ingredients called for in the recipe before you begin. This is known as *mise en place* (see definition at right).

baking is a science

You may have heard the saying, "Baking is a science." In fact, it is. But it's also a great way to learn how to measure and to mix ingredients to create yummy treats like cookies, cakes, and brownies. So roll up your sleeves, and let's start baking!

gather ingredients

Before you start to bake, have all of your tools out and your ingredients measured and ready to use as the recipe directs. The French call this *mise en place*, or "to put in place." Pronounced "meez ahn plahs," this phrase is commonly used in professional kitchens.

shapes & sizes

Ingredients can be cut into different shapes and sizes, such as the ones shown in the photo above:

1 shredded carrots
2 small chunks of pear
3 large chunks of apple
4 strawberries cut in half lengthwise

Use this photo to help you identify the shapes and sizes in the recipes that follow.

measuring

When you bake, it's important to follow the recipe closely and use every ingredient in the correct amount. Just think of how icky cookies would be if they were made with too little sugar or if bread was made with too much salt! Before you get started baking, make sure you have measuring spoons, dry measuring cups, a liquid measuring cup, and a kitchen scale, if weighing dry ingredients. Have a kitchen timer on hand to make sure you don't overbake your cookies or cake.

dry ingredients
Spoon the dry ingredient into a dry measuring cup or onto a scale. Do not pack down the ingredient (unless it's brown sugar, which is measured firmly packed). If using a measuring cup, level off the ingredient with the back of a table knife.

wet ingredients
Put the liquid measuring cup on a flat surface. Bend down so the measuring lines are at eye level. Pour in the liquid until it reaches the correct measuring line.

butter
Use the measuring lines marked on the butter wrapper as your guide. Line up a small, sharp knife on the appropriate measuring line and cut down through the butter to cut off the correct amount.

time
Use a kitchen timer to keep track of time when baking. Don't rely on time alone to know when food is done. Look for the visual cues provided in the recipes.

adding up

dash = 2 or 3 drops

pinch = amount you can pick up between your thumb and forefinger

3 teaspoons = 1 tablespoon

4 tablespoons = about 60 ml (2 fl oz)

for yummy results!

When measuring the ingredients for the recipes in this book, be sure to stick with one system of measurement, either ounces or grams.

preparing baking dishes and pans

1 Rub a piece of butter over the inside of the dish with a paper towel, making a thin, even coating.

2 Sprinkle in some flour, then shake and tilt the dish until it is coated. Turn the dish upside down and tap out the extra flour.

sifting flour (method 1)

1 Put a sifter over a bowl, add the flour, and squeeze the handle to force the flour through the mesh screen.

cracking eggs

1 Gently but firmly tap the middle of the egg on the edge of a bowl to crack the shell.

2 Hold the egg over the bowl and pull the shell halves apart, letting the egg fall into the bowl.

sifting flour (method 2)

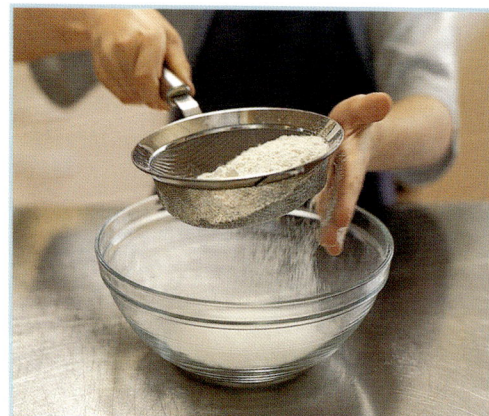

1 Put a fine-mesh sieve over a bowl and add the flour. Hold the sieve by the handle and gently tap it against your other hand.

beating butter and sugar

1 Combine the butter and sugar in a bowl. The butter should be slightly soft for the best results.

2 Using an electric mixer on medium speed, beat the butter and sugar for about 3 minutes, until creamy.

3 Every now and then, stop the mixer and scrape down the sides of the bowl with a rubber spatula.

cutting butter into flour

1 Scatter the butter chunks over the flour. The butter should be very cold for the best results.

2a **Method 1:** Using a pastry blender, make quick chopping motions, pressing down firmly into the butter.

2b **Method 2:** Using 2 table knives, cut through the butter and flour by pulling the knives in opposite directions.

3 The mixture is ready when it looks like coarse crumbs with small pieces of butter still visible.

rinsing fruits

1 Thoroughly rinse all fruits under cool running water. Lay them on a paper towel in an even layer to dry before using.

peeling fruits and vegetables

1 Hold the fruit steady on a cutting board. Using a vegetable peeler, run it down the fruit and away from you.

2 Keep turning and peeling until all the skin is removed.

zesting citrus fruits

1 Using short strokes, rub the citrus fruit over the small holes of a box grater, turning the fruit as you work.

2 Rub off only the colored part of the skin (the zest). Avoid the white part underneath because it tastes bitter.

juicing citrus fruits

1 Hold the fruit on its side on a cutting board and cut it in half. Twist each half over the cone of a juicer, then strain the juice through a fine-mesh sieve.

coring fruits

1 Hold the fruit steady on a cutting board. Using a sharp knife, cut down through the center of the fruit at the stem.

2 Put the fruit halves, cut side down, on the cutting board. Cut each piece in half lengthwise to make quarters.

3 Turn a quarter onto one side and trim away the stem and core. Repeat with the remaining 3 quarters.

hulling (or coring) strawberries

1a **Easy method:** Using a small, sharp knife, cut across the top of the berry, removing the stem.

1b **Advanced method:** Insert the tip of a small, sharp knife near the stem and turn the blade in a circle, removing the stem.

2 Use the strawberries whole or cut lengthwise into halves or slices.

working with puff pastry

1 Thaw the frozen puff pastry unopened in the refrigerator. Gently unfold it on a lightly floured or sugared surface.

2 When not in use, keep the puff pastry covered with a towel so that it doesn't dry out.

3 Roll out the pastry with a rolling pin on the lightly floured or sugared surface.

melting chocolate

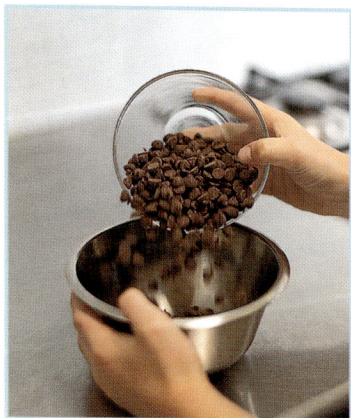

1 Put the chocolate into a heatproof bowl. Select a saucepan in which the bowl will rest comfortably on top. Fill the pan one-third full with water.

2 Heat the water over medium heat until the water is steaming. Place the bowl on top. Make sure the bowl does not touch the water.

3 As the chocolate softens, stir it with a wooden spoon until melted and smooth. Use a pot holder or oven mitt and be careful of the hot steam!

testing for doneness

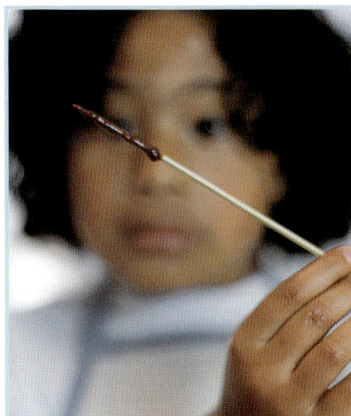

1 Using an oven mitt to steady the pan, poke a wooden skewer or a toothpick into the center of the baked cake or muffin and then pull it straight out.

2 If gooey batter is stuck to the toothpick, the cake or muffin needs to bake longer.

3 If no crumbs are clinging to the toothpick, the cake or muffin is finished baking.

dusting with sugar

1 Put icing sugar in a fine-mesh sieve. Move the sieve slowly over the surface of the baked good while tapping it gently against your other hand.

whipping cream

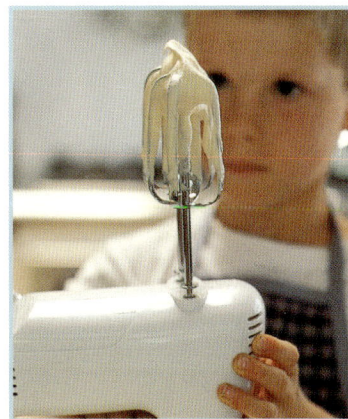

1 Beat the cream with an electric mixer on low speed. Increase the speed to medium-high as the cream thickens. It will take about 3 minutes.

2 Turn off the mixer and lift the beaters. The cream is ready if it stands in medium-firm peaks. Be careful not to beat the cream too long!

cookies

Did you know that a long time ago, sugar was used as medicine?

easy!
peanut butter kiss cookies

makes about **25** cookies

what you need!

ingredients

peanut butter 320 g (11^1/$_4$ oz), at room temperature

light brown sugar 150 g (5^1/$_4$ oz), firmly packed

large egg 1

vanilla essence 1 teaspoon

plain flour 70 g (2^1/$_2$ oz)

chocolate kisses 25, foil removed

tools

measuring cups, spoons, & scale

baking sheet

large mixing bowl

electric mixer

rubber spatula

tablespoon

oven mitts

cooling rack

metal spatula

1 Before you start.

● Preheat the oven to 180°C. Grease the baking sheet with butter.

2 Mix the ingredients.

● In the large bowl, using the electric mixer on medium speed, beat the peanut butter and brown sugar until blended. Turn off the mixer and scrape down the bowl with the rubber spatula.

● Add the egg and vanilla and beat on medium speed until blended. Turn off the mixer and add the flour. Mix on low speed just until blended.

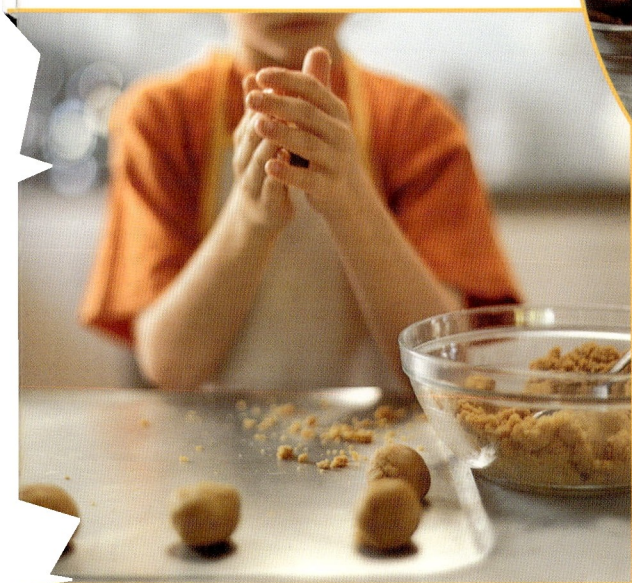

3 Roll the cookies into balls.

● Using the tablespoon, scoop up a rounded spoonful of dough. Scrape the dough off the spoon into the palm of your other hand. Roll the dough into a ball.

● Place the balls on the prepared baking sheet. Repeat, spacing the balls about 4 cm apart.

4 Bake and decorate the cookies.

● Put the baking sheet in the oven and bake the cookies for 10 to 12 minutes, until puffed and dry looking on top. Using oven mitts, remove the baking sheet from the oven and set it on the cooling rack.

● Immediately place an unwrapped chocolate kiss, tip pointing up, in the center of each cookie. Press down slightly to sink the kiss into the cookie. Let the cookies cool on the baking sheet for 10 minutes.

● Move the cookies onto the rack with the metal spatula and let cool completely.

ingredients

ain flour 390 g (13³/4 oz), plus extra
r rolling

aking powder 2¹/2 teaspoons

ound ginger 1 tablespoon

ound cinnamon 1¹/2 teaspoons

ound nutmeg ¹/2 teaspoon

alt ¹/4 teaspoon

utter 115 g (4 oz), at room temperature

ght brown sugar 150 g (5¹/4 oz), firmly
acked

anilla essence 1 teaspoon

arge egg 1

ark molasses 110 g (3³/4 fl oz)

ecorations Decorating Icing (page 25)
nd candies, sultanas, and/or miniature
lain chocolate chips

tools

neasuring cups,
poons, & scale

nedium & large
nixing bowls

vooden spoon

electric mixer

ubber spatula

olastic wrap

3 baking sheets

rolling pin

10-cm kid-shaped
cookie cutter

oven mitts

cooling rack

metal spatula

gingerbread kids

makes about **28** cookies

Note: The dough must be chilled for 1 hour, see step 4.

1 Mix the dry ingredients.

● In the medium bowl, using the wooden spoon, stir together the
flour, baking powder, ginger, cinnamon, nutmeg, and salt.

2 Beat the butter and sugar.

● In the large bowl, using the electric mixer on medium speed, beat
the butter, brown sugar, and vanilla for about 3 minutes, until creamy.

3 Add the egg and molasses.

● Turn off the mixer and scrape down the bowl with the rubber spatula.
Add the egg and molasses and beat on medium speed until blended.

4 Mix the ingredients together.

● Turn off the mixer and add the flour mixture. Mix on low speed just
until blended. The dough will look like moist pebbles.

● Dump the dough onto a work surface and press together into a
solid mound. Divide in half. Press each pile into a flat disk. Wrap each
disk in plastic wrap and refrigerate until well chilled, about 1 hour.

5 Roll out the dough.

• Preheat the oven to 180°C. Grease 3 baking sheets with butter.

• Sprinkle a work surface with some flour. Unwrap 1 chilled disk of dough and place it on the floured surface. Sprinkle the top of the dough with a little flour.

• Roll out the dough with the rolling pin until it is about 6 mm thick (see page 65 for rolling tips). Sprinkle more flour under and over the dough as needed so that it doesn't stick.

6 Cut out shapes.

• Cut a shape out of the dough with the kid-shaped cookie cutter, pressing straight down and lifting straight up. Set the cutout on a baking sheet. Repeat, cutting as close as possible to the previous shape and spacing the cutouts about $2^1/_2$ cm apart on the baking sheet.

• Set the scraps of dough aside and repeat with the second disk of dough.

• Smash all the scraps together, roll the dough out, and cut out more shapes.

decorate with candies, sultanas, or chocolate chips!

7 Bake and cool the cookies.

When 1 baking sheet is full, put it in the oven and bake the cookies for 10 to 12 minutes, until light brown around the edges.

Using oven mitts, remove the baking sheet from the oven and set it on the cooling rack to cool for about 15 minutes.

Move the cookies onto the rack with the metal spatula and let cool completely. Repeat with the rest of the cookies.

8 Decorate the cookies.

● Make the Decorating Icing (see pages 25 and 27). Decorate the cookies with the icing and candies, sultanas, or chocolate chips (see decorating tips on page 28).

easy!
chocolate crinkle cookies

makes about **24** cookies

what you need!

ingredients

icing sugar 60 g (2 oz)

plain flour 230 g (8$^{1}/_{4}$ oz)

unsweetened cocoa powder 40 g (1$^{1}/_{2}$ oz)

baking powder 1$^{1}/_{2}$ teaspoons

salt $^{1}/_{4}$ teaspoon

butter 115 g (4 oz), at room temperature

sugar 250 g (8$^{3}/_{4}$ oz)

large eggs 2

vanilla essence $^{1}/_{2}$ teaspoon

tools

measuring cups, spoons, & scale

2 baking sheets

2 medium & 1 large mixing bowls

wooden spoon

electric mixer

rubber spatula

tablespoon

oven mitts

cooling rack

metal spatula

1 Before you start.

Preheat the oven to 180°C. Grease 2 baking sheets with butter.

Put the icing sugar into one of the medium bowls and set aside.

2 Mix the ingredients.

In the other medium bowl, using the wooden spoon, stir together the flour, cocoa, baking powder, and salt.

In the large bowl, using the electric mixer on medium speed, beat the butter and sugar for about 3 minutes, until creamy. Turn off the mixer and scrape down the bowl with the rubber spatula.

Add 1 egg and beat on medium speed until blended. Add the other egg and vanilla and beat until blended.

Turn off the mixer and add the flour mixture. Mix on low speed just until blended.

3 Form the cookies.

● Using the tablespoon, scoop up a rounded spoonful of dough. Scrape the dough off the spoon into the palm of your other hand. Roll the dough into a ball.

● Roll the ball in the icing sugar until covered. Place the balls on a prepared baking sheet. Repeat, spacing the balls about 5 cm apart.

4 Bake the cookies.

● When 1 baking sheet is full, put it in the oven and bake the cookies for 10 to 12 minutes, until crackled and puffed.

● Using oven mitts, remove the baking sheet from the oven and set it on the cooling rack for 15 minutes.

● Move the cookies onto the rack with the metal spatula and let cool completely. Repeat with the rest of the cookies.

ingredients

COOKIE DOUGH

plain flour 285 g (10 oz), plus extra for rolling

baking powder 1/2 teaspoon

salt 1/4 teaspoon

butter 115 g (4 oz), at room temperature

sugar 200 g (7 oz)

large egg 1

vanilla essence 1 1/2 teaspoons

DECORATING ICING

icing sugar 230 g (8 oz)

warm water 2 tablespoons plus 2 teaspoons

light corn syrup 1 tablespoon

food coloring 2 or 3 drops (optional)

decorations colored sugars, sprinkles, and/or candies

tools

measuring cups, spoons, & scale

2 medium & 1 large mixing bowls

wooden spoon

electric mixer

rubber spatula

plastic wrap

3 baking sheets

rolling pin

6-cm round cookie cutter

oven mitts

cooling rack

metal spatula

whisk (optional)

icing spatula

sugar cookies

makes about **36** cookies

Note: The dough must be chilled for 1 hour, see step 4.

1 Mix the dry ingredients.

● In one of the medium bowls, using the wooden spoon, stir together the flour, baking powder, and salt.

2 Beat the butter and sugar.

● In the large bowl, using the electric mixer on medium speed, beat the butter and sugar for about 3 minutes, until creamy. Turn off the mixer and scrape down the bowl with the rubber spatula.

3 Add the egg and vanilla.

● Add the egg and vanilla and beat on medium speed until blended.

● Turn off the mixer and add the flour mixture. Mix on low speed just until blended. The dough will look lumpy, like moist pebbles.

5 Roll out the dough.

● Preheat the oven to 180°C. Grease 3 baking sheets with butter.

● Sprinkle a work surface with some flour. Unwrap 1 chilled disk of dough and place it on the floured surface. Sprinkle the top of the dough with a little more flour.

● Roll out the dough with the rolling pin until it is about 6 mm thick (see page 65 for rolling tips). Sprinkle more flour under and over the dough as needed so it doesn't stick.

4 Shape the dough.

● Dump the dough onto a work surface and press together into a solid mound. Divide in half. Press each pile into a flat disk. Wrap each disk in plastic wrap and refrigerate until well chilled, about 1 hour.

6 Cut out shapes.

● Cut a shape out of the dough with the round cookie cutter. Set the cutout on a baking sheet.

● Repeat, cutting as close as possible to the previous shape and spacing the cutouts about 2.5 cm apart on the baking sheet.

● Set the scraps of dough aside and repeat with the second chilled disk of dough.

● Smash all the scraps together, roll the dough out, and cut out more shapes.

decorate these cookies with your friends!

7   Bake and cool the cookies.

When 1 baking sheet is full, put it in the oven and bake the cookies for 10 to 12 minutes, until light brown around the edges.

Using oven mitts, remove the baking sheet from the oven and set it on the cooling rack to cool for 15 minutes.

Move the cookies onto the rack with the metal spatula and let cool completely. Repeat with the rest of the cookies.

8   Make the icing.

● In the other medium bowl, using the whisk or the electric mixer on medium-low speed, beat the icing sugar, warm water, and corn syrup until smooth.

● Add the food coloring (if using). You can divide the icing among 2 or 3 small bowls and make each one a different color by adding a few drops of food coloring to each bowl.

● Decorate the cookies (see pages 28 and 29).

decorating cookies

● Using the icing spatula, spread some icing on each of the cookies. Use one or more colors if you want.

● While the icing is soft, decorate the cookies with the colored sugars, sprinkles, and/or candies. The icing must be soft for the decorations to stay in place.

● Set the decorated cookies back on the rack until the icing is firm, about 20 minutes.

how many colors are
on your cookie?

oatmeal-raisin cookies

makes about **24** cookies

what you need!

ingredients

quick-cooking rolled oats 140 g (4^3/$_4$ oz)

plain flour 105 g (3^3/$_4$ oz)

sultanas 50 g (1^3/$_4$ oz)

baking powder ^{1}/$_2$ teaspoon

ground cinnamon ^{1}/$_2$ teaspoon

salt ^{1}/$_4$ teaspoon

butter 115 g (4 oz), at room temperature

light brown sugar 170 g (6 oz), firmly packed

large egg 1

vanilla essence 1 teaspoon

tools

measuring cups, spoons, & scale

2 baking sheets

medium & large mixing bowls

wooden spoon

electric mixer

rubber spatula

2 tablespoons

oven mitts

cooling rack

metal spatula

1 Before you start.

- Preheat the oven to 180°C. Grease 2 baking sheets with butter.

2 Mix the ingredients.

- In the medium bowl, using the wooden spoon, stir together the oats, flour, sultanas, baking powder, cinnamon, and salt.

- In the large bowl, using the electric mixer on medium speed, beat the butter and brown sugar for about 3 minutes, until creamy.

3 Add the egg and vanilla.

- Turn off the mixer and scrape down the bowl with the rubber spatula. Add the egg and vanilla and beat on medium speed until blended.

- Turn off the mixer and add the flour mixture. Mix on low speed just until blended.

4 Form the cookies.

- Using 1 tablespoon, scoop up a heaping spoonful of dough. Using the other tablespoon, push the dough onto a prepared baking sheet. Repeat, spacing the mounds about 4 cm apart.

5 Bake the cookies.

- When 1 baking sheet is full, put it in the oven and bake the cookies for 15 minutes, until puffed and golden brown around the edges.

- Using oven mitts, remove the baking sheet from the oven and set it on the cooling rack to cool for 15 minutes.

- Move the cookies onto the rack with the metal spatula and let cool completely. Repeat with the rest of the cookies.

s'more bars

makes **12** bar cookies

Note: The bars must be chilled for 4 hours before serving.

what you need!

ingredients

butter 3 tablespoons, cut into chunks

whole graham crackers 6

sweetened condensed milk 180 ml (6 fl oz) (not evaporated milk)

plain chocolate chips 250 g (8 oz)

vanilla essence 1 1/2 teaspoons

salt 1 pinch

miniature marshmallows 60 g (2 oz)

graham crackers 2 whole or 90 g (3 oz) mini-graham cracker shapes

tools

measuring cups, spoons, & scale	zippered plastic bag
20-cm square baking pan or dish	rolling pin
aluminum foil	wooden spoon
small & medium saucepans	plastic wrap
pot holder	cutting board
	sharp knife

1 Before you start.

● Line the square baking pan or dish with aluminum foil so that the foil hangs over the sides. Grease the foil with butter.

2 Melt the butter.

● Put the 3 tablespoons of butter in the small saucepan and melt over medium-low heat. Move the pan to a heatproof surface using the pot holder. Let cool for 5 minutes.

3 Crush the crackers and make the crust.

● Put the 6 whole graham crackers into the zippered plastic bag. Press out all the air and seal the bag. Using the rolling pin, gently but firmly crush the cookies to make tiny crumbs. You should have 90 g (3 oz) of crumbs.

● Add the crumbs to the melted butter and stir with the wooden spoon until blended. Scrape the crumbs into the baking pan.

4 Press in the crust.

● Lay a piece of plastic wrap loosely over the crumbs. Place your hand on the plastic wrap and spread the crumbs to coat the bottom of the pan. Once the crumbs are in place, press down firmly to make a solid, even layer. Throw away the plastic wrap when you are finished flattening the crumbs.

5 Make the chocolate filling.

● Heat the condensed milk and chocolate chips in the medium saucepan over medium-low heat, stirring with the wooden spoon until the chocolate is melted and the mixture is smooth. Move the pan to a heatproof surface using the pot holder.

● Add the vanilla and salt. Stir until blended.

● Pour the filling over the graham cracker crust and spread evenly with the spoon.

be careful
when you use
sharp knives!

7 Cut the bars.

● Cover and refrigerate the bars until they are firm, about 4 hours.

● To serve, lift the foil from the pan and set the s'more square on the cutting board. Peel the foil away from the sides, and cut the square into rectangles with the sharp knife. Keep refrigerated until just before serving.

6 Finish the bars.

● Scatter the marshmallows evenly over the chocolate filling and press them in gently.

● If using the 2 whole graham crackers, break them into little pieces. Stick the broken crackers or mini cracker shapes into the filling among the marshmallows.

easy!
fudgy brownie triangles

makes **18** brownie triangles

what you need!

ingredients

butter 170 g (6 oz), cut into chunks

unsweetened chocolate 150 g (5 oz), coarsely chopped

sugar 300 g (10^1/$_2$ oz)

vanilla essence 1^1/$_2$ teaspoons

salt ^{1}/$_4$ teaspoon

large eggs 3

plain flour 140 g (5 oz)

mix-ins 85 g (3 oz) (choose from plain, peanut butter, or white chocolate chips; chopped walnuts or pecans; or candy-coated mini-chocolates)

tools

measuring cups, spoons, & scale

20-cm square baking pan

medium saucepan

wooden spoon

pot holder

medium bowl

oven mitts

cooling rack

sharp knife

metal spatula

1 Before you start.

● Preheat the oven to 180°C. Grease the square baking pan with butter.

2 Melt the butter and chocolate.

● Put the 185 g (6 oz) of butter and the chocolate in the medium saucepan over low heat. Stir with the wooden spoon until melted. Move the pan to a heatproof surface using the pot holder. Scrape the chocolate mixture into the medium bowl and let cool for 5 minutes.

3 Mix the batter.

● Stir the sugar, vanilla, and salt into the cooled chocolate mixture with the wooden spoon.

● Add the eggs one at a time, beating with the wooden spooon after each addition just until mixed.

● Sprinkle the flour over the chocolate mixture and stir until blended. Add the mix-ins and stir just until combined.

4 Fill the pan and bake.

● Scrape the batter into the prepared pan, spreading it evenly with the wooden spoon.

● Put the pan in the oven and bake for 35 to 40 minutes, until the toothpick inserted into the center comes out almost completely clean. Do not overbake or the brownies will be dry.

● Using oven mitts, remove the pan from the oven and set it on the cooling rack to cool completely.

● Cut the brownie into 3 equal strips with the sharp knife, then cut each strip crosswise into 3 equal pieces. Remove the pieces with the metal spatula. Cut each piece into 2 triangles.

cakes & cupcakes

Did you know that people
eat over 600,000 tons
of chocolate every year?

ingredients

VANILLA CAKE

plain flour 320 g (11$\frac{1}{4}$ oz)

baking powder 1 tablespoon

salt $\frac{1}{4}$ teaspoon

butter 170 g (6 oz), at room temperature

sugar 350 g (12$\frac{1}{4}$ oz)

vanilla essence 2 teaspoons

large eggs 3

whole milk 300 ml (10$\frac{1}{2}$ fl oz)

CHOCOLATE FROSTING

plain chocolate chips 170 g (6 oz)

butter 60 g (2 oz), at room temperature

cream cheese 230 g (8 oz), at room temperature

icing sugar 355 g (12$\frac{1}{2}$ oz)

vanilla essence 2 teaspoons

salt $\frac{1}{4}$ teaspoon

double cream 2 tablespoons

decorations candies and sprinkles

tools

measuring cups, spoons, & scale

two 23-cm round cake pans

baking paper, pencil & scissors

sifter

2 medium mixing bowls

electric mixer

rubber spatula

toothpick

oven mitts & cooling racks

small saucepan & heatproof bowl

wooden spoon

icing spatula

birthday cake

makes **12** slices

Note: This is an advanced recipe.

1 Before you start.

● Preheat the oven to 180°C.

● Grease 2 round cake pans with butter.

● Make 2 circles on the piece of baking paper by tracing the bottom of the cake pan. Cut out the circles and press 1 circle into the bottom of each pan. Grease the paper with more butter.

● Sprinkle some flour in each pan and shake and tilt the pans to coat the bottom and sides evenly. Turn the pans upside down and tap out the extra flour (see page 8).

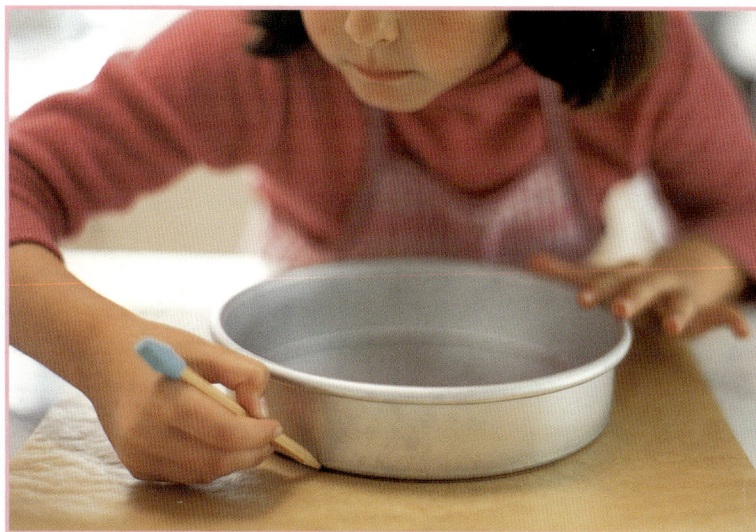

2 Mix the dry ingredients.

● Put the flour, baking powder, and salt into the sifter and sift into one of the medium bowls (see page 8).

3 Make the batter.

- In the large bowl, using the electric mixer on medium speed, beat the butter, sugar, and vanilla for about 3 minutes, until creamy.

- Turn off the mixer and scrape down the bowl with the rubber spatula. Add the eggs one at a time, beating well after each one is added.

- Turn off the mixer, add about one-third of the flour mixture, and mix on low speed just until blended. Pour in half of the milk and mix just until blended.

- Repeat, adding about one-third of the flour, the remaining milk, and then the rest of the flour, mixing after each addition just until blended.

4 Fill the pans.

- Turn off the mixer and scrape down the bowl with the rubber spatula.

- Pour half of the batter into one prepared pan and the other half in the second pan. Using the rubber spatula, spread the batter evenly and smooth the top.

don't forget to lick the frosting off the beaters!

5 Bake and cool the cake.

● Put the pans in the oven and bake for 30 to 35 minutes, until the toothpick inserted into the center of a cake comes out clean. Using oven mitts, remove the pans from the oven and set them on the cooling racks to cool for 20 minutes.

● Turn each pan upside down onto the rack and lift off the pan. Peel off the baking paper and let cool completely.

6 Melt the chocolate.

● Melt the chocolate chips (see page 12) in the heatproof bowl over simmering water, stirring often with the wooden spoon until smooth, about 4 minutes.

● Turn off the heat. Using oven mitts, remove the bowl and set aside to let the chocolate cool slightly.

7 Make the frosting.

● In the other medium bowl, using the electric mixer on medium-low speed, beat the butter and cream cheese until the mixture is smooth and no lumps remain.

● Turn off the mixer and scrape down the bowl with the rubber spatula. Add the icing sugar, vanilla, and salt and beat on low speed until smooth and fluffy.

● Add the chocolate and cream and beat on low until well blended. Decorate the cake (see pages 44 and 45).

decorating a cake

1 Place 1 layer, top side up, on a cake stand or serving plate lined with 5 strips baking or waxed paper.

2 Spread a thick layer of the frosting on top with the icing spatula. Start in the center and move outward.

3 Place the second cake layer on top and press on it gently with your hands to make sure it is level.

4 Spread the rest of the frosting evenly over the top and sides of the cake with the spatula.

5 Carefully remove the paper and decorate the cake with candies, sprinkles, and birthday candles.

6 Have fun decorating with your friends!

7 Serve immediately, or cover loosely and refrigerate up to 3 days. Bring to room temperature before serving.

2

3

6

7

easy!
chocolate chip cookie cake

makes **10** slices

what you need!

ingredients

CHOCOLATE CHIP CAKE

plain flour 140 g (5 oz)

baking powder 1¹/₂ teaspoons

salt ¹/₄ teaspoon

butter 115 g (4 oz), at room temperature

light brown sugar 225 g (8 oz), firmly packed

large egg 1

vanilla essence 1 teaspoon

plain chocolate chips 115 g (4 oz)

TOPPING (OPTIONAL)

whipped cream (see page 69)

strawberries 11, hulled (see page 11)

tools

20-cm round cake pan

small & large mixing bowls

measuring cups, spoons, & scale

wooden spoon

electric mixer

rubber spatula

toothpick

oven mitts

cooling rack

table knife

large spoon

1 Before you start.

● Preheat the oven to 180°C.

● Grease the round cake pan with butter.

● Sprinkle some flour in the pan and shake and tilt the pan to coat the bottom and sides evenly. Turn the pan upside down and tap out the extra flour (see page 8).

2 Make the dough.

● In the small bowl, using the wooden spoon, stir together the flour, baking powder, and salt.

● In the large bowl, using the electric mixer on medium speed, beat the butter and brown sugar for about 3 minutes, until creamy.

● Turn off the mixer and scrape down the bowl with the rubber spatula. Add the egg and vanilla and beat on medium speed until blended.

● Turn off the mixer and add the flour mixture. Mix on low speed just until blended. Using the wooden spoon, stir in the chocolate chips.

3 Fill the pan and bake the cake.

● Scrape the dough into the prepared pan, spreading it evenly with the rubber spatula.

● Put the pan in the oven and bake for 30 minutes, until the toothpick inserted into the center comes out with a few crumbs clinging to it. Using oven mitts, remove the pan from the oven and set it on the cooling rack to cool for 30 minutes. Run the knife around the edge to loosen.

4 Decorate the cake.

● Place a plate upside down on top of the cake. Turn the cake and the plate right side up and lift off the pan.

● If adding the topping, make the Whipped Cream (see page 69). Mound the cream on top of the cake with the large spoon and spread evenly. Place 10 strawberries around the rim, with 1 in the center.

ingredients

CARROT CAKE

carrots 2 medium

plain flour 215 g (7$^{1}/_{2}$ oz)

light brown sugar 225 g (8 oz), firmly packed

baking powder 2 teaspoons

ground cinnamon $^{3}/_{4}$ teaspoon

salt $^{1}/_{4}$ teaspoon

vegetable oil 120 ml (4 fl oz)

large eggs 3

vanilla essence 1 teaspoon

walnuts 60 g (2 oz) chopped (optional)

sultanas 30 g (1 oz) (optional)

CREAM CHEESE FROSTING

butter 30 g (1 oz), at room temperature

cream cheese 115 g (4 oz), at room temperature

icing sugar 140 g (5 oz)

vanilla essence 1 teaspoon

salt $^{1}/_{4}$ teaspoon

tools

measuring cups, spoons, & scale	wooden spoon
	rubber spatula
20-cm square baking pan	toothpick
vegetable peeler	oven mitts
box grater-shredder	cooling rack
2 medium & 1 large mixing bowls	electric mixer
	icing spatula

carrot cake

makes **9** slices

1 Before you start.

● Preheat the oven to 165°C.

● Grease the square baking pan with butter.

2 Shred the carrots.

● Peel the carrots with the vegetable peeler (see page 10).

● Hold the box grater-shredder firmly on a work surface with 1 hand. Use your other hand to slide each carrot over the large holes to create shreds. Keep your fingers away from the holes!

● Measure 155 g (5 oz) and set aside.

3 Make the batter.

● In the large bowl, using the wooden spoon, stir together the flour, brown sugar, baking powder, cinnamon, and salt.

● In one of the medium bowls, using the wooden spoon, stir together the carrots, oil, eggs, and vanilla.

● Pour the carrot mixture into the flour mixture. Add the walnuts and sultanas (if using). Stir just until blended. Scrape the batter into the prepared pan, spreading it evenly with the rubber spatula.

4 Bake the cake.

● Put the pan in the oven and bake for about 40 minutes, until the toothpick inserted into the center comes out clean.

● Using oven mitts, remove the pan from the oven and set it on the cooling rack to cool for 5 minutes.

5 Cool the cake.

● Using oven mitts, remove the pan from the cooling rack and place it on a heatproof surface. Place the cooling rack upside down on top of the cake.

● Turn the cake and rack over so that the cake is upside down on the cooling rack.

● Lift off the pan and let the cake cool completely.

for extra yumminess, spread on the frosting extra thick!

6 Make the frosting.

● In the other medium bowl, using the electric mixer on medium-low speed, beat the butter and cream cheese until the mixture is smooth and no lumps remain.

● Turn off the mixer and scrape down the bowl with the rubber spatula. Add the icing sugar, vanilla, and salt and beat on low speed until smooth and fluffy.

7 Frost the cake.

● Place the cooled cake, top side up, on a serving plate.

● Spread a thick layer of frosting over the top of the cake with the icing spatula. Serve at room temperature.

coconut cupcakes

makes **12** cupcakes

ingredients

CUPCAKES

plain flour 250 g (8³/₄ oz)

baking powder 1¹/₂ teaspoons

salt ¹/₄ teaspoon

butter 115 g (4 oz), at room temperature

sugar 200 g (7 oz)

vanilla essence 1 teaspoon

large eggs 2, at room temperature

yogurt 115 g (4 oz) plain (unflavored)

coconut 40 g (1¹/₂ oz) sweetened, shredded

VANILLA FROSTING

butter 170 g (6 oz), at room temperature

icing sugar 370 g (13 oz)

double cream 2 tablespoons

vanilla essence 2 teaspoons

salt ¹/₄ teaspoon

COCONUT TOPPING

coconut 170 g (6 oz) sweetened, shredded

tools

measuring cups, spoons, & scale

12-cup muffin pan

muffin-cup liners

2 medium & 1 large mixing bowls

wooden spoon

electric mixer

rubber spatula

2 large spoons

toothpick

oven mitts

cooling rack

shallow bowl

small icing spatula

1 Before you start.

● Preheat the oven to 190°C. Line the muffin pan with liners.

2 Mix the batter.

● In one of the medium bowls, using the wooden spoon, stir together the flour, baking powder, and salt.

● In the large bowl, using the electric mixer on medium speed, beat the butter, sugar, and vanilla for about 3 minutes, until creamy. Add the eggs one at a time, beating well after each one is added. Turn off the mixer and scrape down the bowl with the rubber spatula.

● Add half of the flour mixture, and mix on low speed just until blended. Add the yogurt and mix until smooth. Add the rest of the flour mixture and coconut and mix just until blended. Turn off the mixer and scrape down the bowl with the rubber spatula.

3 Fill the cups.

● Using the 2 large spoons, one to scoop and one to push, fill each lined cup mostly full with batter.

4 Bake and cool the cupcakes.

● Put the pan in the oven and bake about 25 minutes, until the toothpick inserted into the center of a cupcake comes out clean.

● Using oven mitts, remove the pan from the oven and set on the cooling rack for 20 minutes. Tip the cupcakes out of the pan onto the rack and let cool completely.

5 Frost and decorate the cupcakes.

● In the other medium bowl, using the electric mixer on low speed, beat together the butter, icing sugar, cream, vanilla, and salt for 3 minutes, until smooth.

● Pour the 170 g (6 oz) coconut into the shallow bowl.

● Frost the top of each cupcake with the icing spatula, mounding it in the center. Holding the bottom of each cupcake, roll the frosted top in the coconut.

ingredients

CHOCOLATE CAKE
plain flour 140 g (5 oz)

unsweetened cocoa powder 20 g (^{3}/4 oz)

baking powder 2 teaspoons

salt 1/4 teaspoon

sugar 150 g (5^1/4 oz)

warm water 175 ml (6 fl oz)

large egg 1

vegetable oil 75 ml (2^1/2 fl oz)

vanilla essence 1 tablespoon

ICE CREAM LAYER
ice cream 1/2 gallon (2 L) (choose your favorite flavor: peppermint, vanilla, mint chocolate chip, or chocolate)

WHIPPED CREAM
double cream 350 ml (12 fl oz), well chilled

sugar 3 tablespoons

vanilla essence 1 teaspoon

TOPPING
hard peppermint candies 15 (70 g/2^1/2 oz)

tools

measuring cups, spoons, & scale	toothpick
	oven mitts
23-by-33-cm glass baking dish	cooling rack
sifter	electric mixer
1 large & 2 medium mixing bowls	zippered plastic bag
whisk	rolling pin
rubber spatula	large knife
	metal spatula

ice cream cake

makes **12** slices

Note: This is an advanced recipe and takes extra time, see step 4.

1 Before you start.

● Preheat the oven to 165°C. Grease the baking dish with butter.

2 Make the batter.

● Put the flour, cocoa, baking powder, and salt into the sifter and sift into the large bowl (see page 8). Stir in the sugar with the whisk.

● In one of the medium bowls, using the whisk, beat the water, egg, oil, and vanilla until blended. Pour the egg mixture into the flour mixture and stir together with the whisk just until blended.

3 Fill the dish and bake the cake.

● Pour the batter into the prepared dish. Use the rubber spatula to scrape all of the batter out of the bowl into the dish.

● Put the dish in the oven and bake for about 20 minutes, until the toothpick inserted into the center comes out clean.

● Using oven mitts, remove the dish from the oven and set it on the cooling rack to cool completely.

be careful not to beat the whipped cream too long!

4 Spread on the ice cream layer.

● When the cake is cool, remove the ice cream from the freezer and set it on the counter to soften for 10 to 15 minutes.

● Drop large globs of the ice cream over the top of the cake with the rubber spatula and spread them out to make a thick, even layer.

● Cover with plastic wrap and freeze for about 4 hours, until the ice cream is hard.

5 Make the whipped cream.

● In the other medium bowl, using the electric mixer on low speed, beat the cream, sugar, and vanilla.

● When the cream begins to thicken and no longer splatters, increase the speed to medium-high.

● Continue to beat until medium-firm peaks form, about 3 minutes (see page 13).

6 Crush the candies.

● Unwrap the peppermint candies and throw away the plastic wrappers. Put the candies into the zippered plastic bag. Press out all the air and seal the bag.

● Using the rolling pin, gently but firmly pound on the candies until they are crushed.

● Remove the frozen cake from the freezer.

7 Decorate the cake.

● Spread the whipped cream evenly over the frozen cake with the rubber spatula, then sprinkle with the crushed candies.

● Cut into 12 squares with the large knife. Remove from the pan with the metal spatula. Serve immediately or store in the freezer.

ingredients

CRUST

butter 115 g (4 oz), cut into chunks

graham cracker crumbs 135 g (4¹/₂ oz) (9 crackers; see step 3, page 33)

sugar 3 tablespoons

FILLING

cream cheese 230 g (8 oz), at room temperature

plain flour 2 tablespoons

salt ¹/₄ teaspoon

sugar 250 g (8³/₄ oz)

sour cream 125 g (4 oz)

vanilla essence 1 tablespoon

large eggs 3

TOPPING

strawberries 500 g (1 lb), hulled and cut in half lengthwise (see page 11)

tools

measuring cups, spoons, & scale	medium & large mixing bowls
small saucepan	electric mixer
wooden spoon	rubber spatula
pot holder	oven mitts
23-cm springform pan	cooling rack
plastic wrap	long, thin metal spatula

strawberry cheesecake

makes **16** slices

Note: The cheesecake must be chilled overnight before serving.

1 Make the crust.

● Put the butter in the small saucepan and melt over medium-low heat. Move the pan to a heatproof surface using the pot holder. Using the wooden spoon, stir in the crumbs and sugar. Scrape the crumbs into the springform pan.

● Lay a piece of plastic wrap loosely over the crumbs. Place your hand on the plastic wrap and spread the crumbs evenly over the bottom and 5 cm up the sides of the pan. Press down firmly to make a solid, even layer. Throw away the plastic wrap when you are finished. Refrigerate the crust while you make the filling.

2 Make the filling.

● Preheat the oven to 150°C.

● In the large bowl, using the electric mixer on medium speed, beat the cream cheese, flour, and salt for about 3 minutes, until fluffy and smooth. Turn off the mixer and scrape down the bowl with the rubber spatula.

● Add the sugar, sour cream, and vanilla. Beat on medium-high speed until smooth. Stop and scrape down the bowl again. Add the eggs one at a time, beating well on medium-high speed after each one is added.

3 Bake and cool the cheesecake.

● Remove the crust from the refrigerator and pour the filling into it. Put the pan in the oven and bake for 65 to 70 minutes. To test for doneness, using oven mitts, nudge the pan; the center of the cake should jiggle slightly.

● Using oven mitts, remove the pan from the oven and set it on the cooling rack to cool completely. Cover with plastic wrap and refrigerate until cold (overnight is best).

4 Serve the cheesecake.

● Loosen the clasp on the pan sides and remove the sides. Slip the metal spatula between the crust and the pan bottom and slide the cake onto a serving plate.

● Arrange the strawberry halves on top of the cheesecake. Serve immediately.

pies & pastries

Did you know that the strawberry is the only fruit with seeds on the outside?

ingredients

DOUGH

plain flour 355 g (12$\frac{1}{2}$ oz), plus extra for rolling

sugar 2 tablespoons

salt $\frac{1}{2}$ teaspoon

very cold unsalted butter 170 g (6 oz), cut into chunks

very cold water 120 ml (4 fl oz)

FILLING

mixed berries 680 g (24 oz), such as blackberries, blueberries, and strawberries

sugar 150 g (5$\frac{1}{4}$ oz)

cornflour 30 g (1 oz)

salt $\frac{1}{4}$ teaspoon

ground cinnamon 1 pinch

ground nutmeg 1 pinch

vanilla essence $\frac{1}{2}$ teaspoon

TOPPING

large egg 1, beaten

sugar 2 tablespoons

tools

measuring cups, spoons, & scale

2 large mixing bowls

wooden spoon

pastry blender or 2 table knives

plastic wrap

small knife

rolling pin

23-cm glass pie dish

ruler

pizza wheel

table fork

pastry brush

baking sheet

oven mitts

cooling rack

mixed berry pie

makes **6 to 8** slices

Note: This is an advanced recipe and takes extra time, see step 3.

1 Mix the dry ingredients.

● In one of the large bowls, using the wooden spoon, stir together the flour, sugar, and salt.

2 Make the dough.

● Scatter the butter over the flour mixture. Cut the butter into the flour with the pastry blender or 2 table knives (see page 9). The mixture is ready when it looks like coarse crumbs with small pieces of butter still visible.

● Drizzle the cold water over the dough and stir gently with the wooden spoon until the mixture forms moist crumbs.

mix the berries gently so they don't get smushed!

3 Shape the dough.

● Dump the crumbs onto a work surface and press together into a solid mound.

● Divide the mound in half. Press each pile into a flat disk.

● Wrap each disk in plastic wrap and refrigerate until well chilled, about 30 minutes or for up to 2 days.

4 Make the filling.

● If using, hull the strawberries with the small knife (see page 11). Cut in half lengthwise.

● In the other large bowl, using the wooden spoon, stir together the berries, sugar, cornflour, salt, cinnamon, nutmeg, and vanilla. Set aside.

● Preheat the oven to 200°C.

5 Roll out the dough.

● Sprinkle a work surface with some flour. Unwrap 1 chilled disk of dough and place it on the floured surface. Sprinkle the top of the dough with a little more flour.

● Roll out the dough with the rolling pin until it is about 3 mm thick. Stop a few times and lift and turn the dough so that it becomes a circle. Sprinkle more flour under and over the dough as needed so it doesn't stick. The circle should be about 35 cm across when you finish.

6 Line the dish with dough.

● Move the pie dish close to the dough circle.

● Loosely roll the dough around the rolling pin.

● Lift the rolling pin over the dish and slowly unroll the dough into the dish. It will hang over the edges.

● Gently press the dough into the dish with your fingertips. Cover loosely with plastic wrap and refrigerate while you cut out the lattice strips.

7 Cut out the lattice strips.

● Sprinkle a little flour on the work surface. Unwrap the second disk of dough and place it on the floured surface. Sprinkle the top of the dough with a little more flour.

● Roll out the dough as you did for the bottom crust until you have a large rectangle about 23 by 35 cm.

● Using the ruler and the pizza wheel or the small knife, cut 8 strips, each about 35 cm long and 2^1/$_2$ cm wide.

8 Lay strips across the filling.

● Remove the pastry-lined pie dish from the refrigerator and remove the plastic wrap.

● Using the wooden spoon, gently stir the berry filling again. Pile the filling into the dish.

● Lay 4 of the lattice strips horizontally across the pie.

line up the dough strips in neat rows!

9 Finish the lattice top.

● Lay the remaining 4 lattice strips vertically over the bottom strips.

● Cut away the extra dough with the small knife, leaving a 2.5-cm overhang.

● Fold the overhang under itself so that it rests on top of the rim of the dish.

10 Crimp the edge and bake.

● Crimp the edge of the pie with the fork by pressing the tines of the fork gently around the border.

● Use the pastry brush to brush the lattice strips and crimped border with the beaten egg. Sprinkle the top of the lattice strips with the sugar.

● Put the pie on the baking sheet, put in the oven, and bake the pie for about 50 minutes, until the crust is golden brown and the berry juices are bubbling. Using oven mitts, carefully remove the baking sheet and pie from the oven and set it on the cooling rack. Let the pie cool completely before slicing.

cherry crisp

makes **6** servings

ingredients

TOPPING

butter 60 g (2 oz), at room temperature

light brown sugar 60 g (2 oz), firmly packed

ground cinnamon $^1/_2$ teaspoon

salt 1 pinch

old-fashioned rolled oats 35 g (1$^1/_4$ oz)

plain flour 45 g (1$^1/_2$ oz)

walnuts or pecans 60 g (2 oz) chopped (optional)

FILLING

cherries 900 g (1 kg) fresh or thawed frozen

dried tart cherries 60 g (2 oz)

vanilla essence 1 teaspoon

sugar 125 g (4 oz)

plain flour 1 tablespoon

salt 1 pinch

WHIPPED CREAM

double cream 125 ml (4 fl oz), well chilled

sugar 1 tablespoon

vanilla essence $^1/_4$ teaspoon

tools

measuring cups, spoons, & scale

2 medium & 1 large mixing bowls

wooden spoon

plastic wrap

2-litre glass baking dish

cherry pitter

oven mitts

cooling rack

electric mixer

1 Make the topping.

● In one of the medium bowls, using the wooden spoon, stir together the butter, brown sugar, cinnamon, and salt until blended. Stir in the oats, flour, and nuts (if using).

● Cover with plastic wrap and refrigerate while you make the filling.

● Preheat the oven to 190°C. Butter the baking dish.

3 Assemble and bake the crisp.

● Spoon the cherry mixture into the prepared baking dish and spread evenly.

● Remove the topping from the refrigerator and sprinkle it evenly over the fruit.

● Put the dish in the oven and bake for 30 to 35 minutes, until the filling is bubbling and the topping is brown. Using oven mitts, remove the dish from the oven and set it on the cooling rack to cool for 20 minutes.

2 Make the filling.

● If using fresh cherries, remove the stems and pit them with the cherry pitter. If using frozen cherries, pat dry.

● In the large bowl, using the wooden spoon, stir together the cherries, dried cherries, and vanilla. Sprinkle the sugar, flour, and salt over the cherry mixture and stir together gently with the wooden spoon.

4 Make the whipped cream.

● In the other medium bowl, using the electric mixer on low speed, beat the cream, sugar, and vanilla. When the cream begins to thicken and no longer splatters, increase the speed to medium-high. Continue to beat until medium-firm peaks form, about 3 minutes (see page 13).

● To serve, scoop up portions of the warm crisp onto dessert plates. Top each serving with whipped cream.

ingredients

FILLING

apples 2, about 375 g (12 oz) total

pear 1, about 250 g (8 oz), firm but ripe

light brown sugar 75 g (2¹/2 oz), firmly packed

plain flour 1 tablespoon

vanilla essence ¹/2 teaspoon

ground cinnamon ¹/2 teaspoon

ground nutmeg 1 pinch

sultanas 60 g (2 oz) (optional)

PASTRY

plain flour for rolling

frozen puff pastry 2 sheets, each 24 cm square, thawed

large egg 1, beaten

sugar 2 tablespoons

tools

measuring cups, spoons, & scale	rolling pin
2 baking sheets	ruler
medium and small mixing bowls	pizza wheel or table knife
small, sharp knife	table fork
vegetable peeler	pastry brush
cutting board	oven mitts
wooden spoon	cooling racks

apple-pear turnovers

makes **8** large turnovers

1 Before you start.

● Position 2 oven racks evenly in the oven near the center so there is space in between them. Preheat the oven to 200°C.

● Grease 2 baking sheets with butter.

2 Make the filling.

● Peel, cut into quarters, and core the apples and the pear (see pages 10 and 11).

● Using the small, sharp knife, cut the apple and pear quarters into small chunks.

● Put the chunks into the medium bowl. Add the brown sugar, flour, vanilla, cinnamon, nutmeg, and sultanas (if using) and stir together with the wooden spoon.

3 Roll out the pastry.

● Sprinkle a work surface with some flour. Unfold 1 of the thawed puff pastry sheets on top of the flour. Keep the other sheet wrapped in the refrigerator.

● Sprinkle some flour on the pastry. Using the rolling pin, and beginning at the center of the pastry, roll out to the far side. Then, roll from the center toward you. After every few rolls, give the pastry a quarter turn and sprinkle the top and bottom of the pastry with more of the flour so the pastry does not stick. Keep rolling and sprinkling until the pastry is a 31^3/$_4$-cm square.

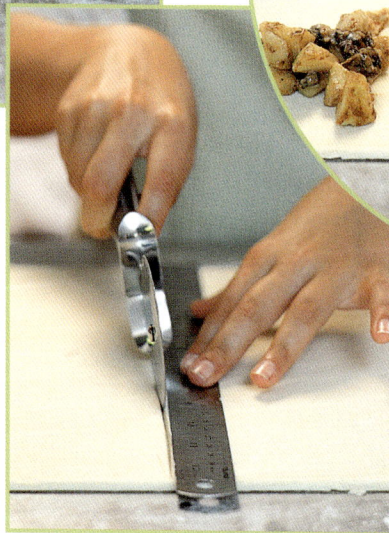

4 Cut out the squares.

● Using the ruler and the pizza wheel or table knife, trim the edges to make a 30-cm square. Pull away the scraps of dough and discard.

● Cut the 30-cm square into four equal 15-cm squares.

5 Add the filling.

● Spoon 75 g (2^3/$_4$ oz) of the filling into the center of each square. Spread the filling across the middle toward 2 opposite points.

● In the small bowl, beat the egg with the fork. Set aside.

make sure to seal the edges so the filling doesn't ooze out!

6 Assemble the turnovers.

● Brush the beaten egg along 2 edges of each square with the pastry brush.

● Fold one-half of each square over the filling, enclosing it fully and forming a triangle. Press the edges together with the fork to seal them.

● Place the 4 turnovers on a prepared baking sheet, spacing them 5 cm apart. Repeat with the remaining puff pastry sheet and filling.

7 Brush and bake the turnovers.

● Use the pastry brush to brush the tops of the turnovers with the beaten egg. Sprinkle the turnovers with the sugar.

● Put one baking sheet on the upper rack in the oven and the other sheet on the lower rack in the oven and bake for 10 minutes. Then, using oven mitts, remove the baking sheets and put each one on the opposite rack. Bake for 15 minutes more, until puffed and brown.

● Using oven mitts, remove the baking sheets from the oven and set each on a cooling rack to cool for 10 minutes.

elephant ears

makes about **20** pastries

what you need!

ingredients

butter 30 g (1 oz), cut into chunks

vanilla essence 1/2 teaspoon

sugar 125 g (4 oz)

icing sugar 60 g (2 oz)

frozen puff pastry 1 sheet, 24 cm square, thawed

tools

measuring cups, spoons, & scale	table fork
2 baking sheets	rolling pin
baking paper	ruler
small & medium saucepans	pastry brush
pot holder	cutting board
wooden spoon	sharp knife
small mixing bowl	oven mitts
	cooling racks
	metal spatula

1 Before you start.

- Preheat the oven to 190°C.
- Line 2 baking sheets with baking paper.

2 Melt the butter.

- Put the butter in the small saucepan and melt over medium-low heat. Move the pan to a heatproof surface using the pot holder. Using the wooden spoon, stir in the vanilla. Set aside to cool slightly.

3 Prepare the pastry.

- In the small bowl, using the fork, stir together the 2 sugars. Measure out 125 g (4 oz) of the sugar mixture and set aside.

- Sprinkle about 3 tablespoons of the remaining sugar mixture on a work surface. Unfold the thawed puff pastry on top of the sugar. Sprinkle more of the sugar mixture on top of the pastry, spreading it out evenly with your hands.

paint the butter onto the pastry with a pastry brush!

4 Roll out the pastry.

● Using the rolling pin and beginning at the center of the pastry, roll out to the far side. Then, roll from the center toward you.

● After every few rolls, sprinkle the top and bottom of the pastry with more of the sugar mixture so the pastry does not stick. Keep rolling and sprinkling until the pastry is a 25-by-50-cm rectangle.

5 Brush and sugar the pastry.

● Brush the cooled melted butter evenly over the pastry with the pastry brush.

● Sprinkle the reserved 125 g (4 oz) sugar mixture and any extra sugar left over from rolling over the pastry. Spread the sugar mixture out evenly with your hands to cover the pastry.

6 Fold the pastry.

● Starting at one short end, fold a 5-cm-wide band of the pastry over onto itself. Repeat this folding until you reach the center of the pastry (about 3 folds).

● Now fold the other end of the rectangle in toward the center in the same way.

● Fold one band on top of the other to form a long rectangle about 6 cm wide and 25 cm long. Press down on the rectangle with the palms of your hands to make the 2 bands stick together.

7 Slice the pastry.

● Put the rectangle on a cutting board. Cut the rectangle crosswise into 12-mm-thick slices with a sharp knife. You should have about 20 slices. Place the slices, cut side down, on the prepared baking sheets, spacing them about 5 cm apart.

8 Bake the pastries.

● Put 1 baking sheet in the oven and bake for about 15 minutes, until brown. Using oven mitts, remove the baking sheet from the oven and set it on one of the cooling racks to cool for 10 minutes.

● Bake the remaining pastries.

● After the pastries cool for 10 minutes, move them onto the rack with the metal spatula and let cool completely.

ingredients

DOUGH

plain flour 180 g (6¼ oz), plus extra for rolling

sugar 1 tablespoon

salt ¼ teaspoon

very cold unsalted butter 85 g (3 oz), cut into chunks

very cold water 60 ml (2 fl oz)

FILLING

tart apples 905 g (32 oz), such as Granny Smith or pippin

light brown sugar 75 g (2½ oz), firmly packed

plain flour 35 g (1¼ oz)

ground cinnamon ¾ teaspoon

ground nutmeg 1 pinch

vanilla essence ½ teaspoon

TOPPING

sugar 2 tablespoons

tools

measuring cups, spoons, & scale	cutting board
2 large mixing bowls	small, sharp knife
	baking sheet
wooden spoon	baking paper
pastry blender or 2 table knives	rolling pin
	table fork
plastic wrap	oven mitts
vegetable peeler	cooling rack

apple galette

makes **6 to 8** slices

Note: This is an advanced recipe and takes extra time, see step 2.

1 Make the dough.

● In one of the large bowls, using the wooden spoon, stir together the flour, sugar, and salt.

● Scatter the butter over the flour mixture. Cut the butter into the flour with the pastry blender or 2 table knives (see page 9). The mixture is ready when it looks like coarse crumbs with small pieces of butter still visible.

● Drizzle the cold water over the dough and stir gently with the wooden spoon until the mixture forms moist crumbs.

2 Shape the dough.

● Dump the crumbs onto a work surface and press into a flat disk.

● Wrap the disk in plastic wrap and refrigerate until well chilled, about 30 minutes or for up to 2 days.

3 Make the filling.

● Peel, cut into quarters, and core the apples (see pages 10 and 11).

● Using the small, sharp knife, cut the apple quarters into medium chunks.

● Put the apple chunks into the other large bowl. Add the brown sugar, flour, cinnamon, nutmeg, and vanilla and stir together with the wooden spoon.

4 Roll out the dough.

● Preheat the oven to 200°C. Line the baking sheet with baking paper.

● Sprinkle a work surface with some flour. Unwrap the chilled disk of dough and place it on the floured surface. Sprinkle the top of the dough with a little more flour.

● Roll out the dough with the rolling pin until it is about 3 mm thick. Stop a few times and lift and turn the dough so that it becomes a circle. Sprinkle more flour under and over the dough as needed so it doesn't stick. The circle should be about 35 cm across when you finish.

pat down the apples into a thick even layer!

5 Add the apples.

● Move the prepared baking sheet close to the dough circle.

● Loosely roll the dough around the rolling pin.

● Lift the rolling pin over the baking sheet and slowly unroll the dough onto the sheet.

● Pile the apple filling onto the center of the dough, leaving a border of dough about 7.5 cm wide.

6 Finish and bake the galette.

● Using your fingers, gently fold the border of dough up and over the filling, folding the dough all around the edge as you go. The center of the galette will be open. Sprinkle the edges of the dough with the sugar.

● Put the baking sheet in the oven and bake for 50 to 55 minutes, until the crust is golden brown and the apple chunks are tender. To test if the apples are done, poke the fork into a chunk. The fork should go in and out easily.

● Using oven mitts, remove the baking sheet from the oven and set it on the cooling rack to cool completely.

simple breads & muffins

Did you know that different types of bananas can be yellow, red, and even blue?

easy!
banana bread

makes **1** loaf

what you need!

 ### ingredients

plain flour 230 g (8^1/$_4$ oz)

baking powder 2 teaspoons

salt ^{1}/$_2$ teaspoon

bicarbonate of soda ^{1}/$_4$ teaspoon

bananas 3 medium, very ripe, peeled

sugar 130 g (4^1/$_2$ oz)

vegetable oil 75 ml (2^1/$_2$ fl oz)

large eggs 2

vanilla essence 1^1/$_2$ teaspoons

 ### tools

measuring cups, spoons, & scale

21^1/$_2$-by-11^1/$_2$-cm metal loaf pan

medium & large mixing bowls

wooden spoon

table fork & table knife

toothpick

oven mitts

cooling rack

1 Before you start.

- Preheat the oven to 180°C.
- Grease the loaf pan with butter.

2 Make the batter.

- In the medium bowl, using the wooden spoon, stir together the flour, baking powder, salt, and bicarbonate of soda.
- In the large bowl, smash the bananas with the fork. Add the sugar, oil, eggs, and vanilla and beat with the wooden spoon until well blended.
- Add the flour mixture to the banana mixture. Stir just until blended.

3 Bake the bread.

- Scrape the batter into the prepared pan, spreading it evenly with the wooden spoon.
- Put the pan in the oven and bake for about 45 minutes, until the toothpick inserted into the center of the bread comes out with just a few crumbs clinging to it.
- Using oven mitts, remove the pan from the oven and set it on a rack to cool for 20 minutes.

4 Remove the bread from the pan.

- Gently run the table knife along the inside edge of the pan to loosen the bread from the sides.
- Using oven mitts, turn the pan on its side and slip the loaf out onto the cooling rack. Let the loaf cool for 15 minutes before serving.

easy!
chocolate chip muffins

makes **12** muffins

what you need!

ingredients

plain flour 355 g (12^1/$_2$ oz)

baking powder 3^1/$_2$ teaspoons

salt ^{1}/$_2$ teaspoon

butter 170 g (6 oz), at room temperature

sugar 200 g (7 oz) plus 1 tablespoon

large eggs 2, at room temperature

vanilla essence 1^1/$_2$ teaspoons

whole milk 175 ml (6 fl oz)

plain chocolate chips 115 g (4 oz)

tools

measuring cups, spoons, & scale

12-cup muffin pan

muffin-cup liners

medium & large mixing bowls

wooden spoon

electric mixer

rubber spatula

2 large spoons

toothpick

oven mitts

cooling rack

1 Before you start.

- Preheat the oven to 180°C.

- Line the muffin pan with muffin-cup liners.

2 Mix the batter.

- In the medium bowl, using the wooden spoon, stir together the flour, baking powder, and salt.

- In the large bowl, using the electric mixer on medium speed, beat the butter and 200 g (7oz) sugar for about 3 minutes, until creamy. Turn off the mixer and scrape down the bowl with the rubber spatula.

- Add 1 egg and beat until blended. Add the other egg and the vanilla and beat until well blended. Turn off the mixer and scrape down the bowl with the rubber spatula.

- Add half of the flour mixture and mix on low speed just until blended. Pour in the milk and mix just until blended. Add the rest of the flour and the chocolate chips and mix until blended.

3 Fill the cups.

- Using the 2 large spoons, one to scoop and one to push, fill each lined cup mostly full with batter. Sprinkle the 1 tablespoon sugar evenly over the tops.

4 Bake the muffins.

- Put the pan in the oven and bake for 21 to 23 minutes, until the muffins are golden brown and the toothpick inserted into the center of a muffin comes out clean.

- Using oven mitts, remove the pan from the oven and set it on the cooling rack to cool for 20 minutes.

- Tip the muffins out of the pan onto the rack and serve warm or at room temperature.

blueberry-orange mini muffins

makes **24** mini muffins

what you need!

ingredients

butter 85 g (3 oz), cut into chunks

plain flour 215 g (7^1/$_2$ oz)

sugar 65 g (2^1/$_4$ oz) plus 2 tablespoons

baking powder 2^1/$_4$ teaspoons

salt ^{1}/$_4$ teaspoon

whole milk 150 ml (5^1/$_4$ fl oz)

large egg 1, at room temperature

orange zest 1 teaspoon finely grated
(see page 10)

vanilla essence ^{1}/$_2$ teaspoon

blueberries 100 g (3^1/$_2$ oz) fresh

tools

measuring cups,
spoons, & scale

small saucepan

pot holder

24-cup mini-muffin
pan

mini-muffin-cup
liners

medium & small
mixing bowls

wooden spoon

2 large spoons

toothpick

oven mitts

cooling racks

1 Melt the butter.

● Put the butter in the small saucepan and melt over medium-low heat. Move the pan to a heatproof surface using the pot holder. Let cool for 5 minutes.

● Preheat the oven to 190°C. Line the mini muffin pan with liners.

2 Mix the batter.

● In the medium bowl, using the wooden spoon, stir together the flour, 65 g (2¼ oz) sugar, baking powder, and salt.

● In the small bowl, using the wooden spoon, beat together the milk, egg, orange zest, and vanilla. Stir in the blueberries. Add the milk mixture and melted butter to the flour mixture. Stir gently just until blended.

3 Fill the cups and bake.

● Using the 2 large spoons, one to scoop and one to push, fill each lined cup mostly full with batter. Sprinkle the 2 tablespoons sugar evenly over the tops.

● Put the pan in the oven and bake for 12 to 15 minutes, until the muffins are golden brown and the toothpick inserted into the center of a muffin comes out clean.

● Using oven mitts, remove the pan from the oven and set it on the cooling rack to cool for 15 minutes.

● Tip the muffins out of the pan onto the rack and serve warm or at room temperature.

simple breads & muffins 89

puffy apple oven pancake

makes **8** servings

what you need!

ingredients

apple 1 small

sugar 4 tablespoons

ground cinnamon ¹/₂ teaspoon

large eggs 3, at room temperature

whole milk 245 ml (80 fl oz), at room temperature

plain flour 105 g (3³/₄ oz)

vanilla essence ³/₄ teaspoon

icing sugar 2 tablespoons

tools

measuring cups, spoons, & scale

23-cm glass pie dish

vegetable peeler

cutting board

small, sharp knife

small mixing bowl

table fork

electric blender

oven mitts

cooling rack

fine-mesh sieve

1 Before you start.

● Preheat the oven to 200°C. Grease the pie dish with butter.

2 Prepare the apple.

● Peel, cut into quarters, and core the apple (see pages 10 and 11).

● Using the small knife, cut the apple quarters into small chunks.

keep your hand
on the lid so
it stays on tight!

3 Make the apple filling.

● In the small bowl, using the fork, stir together
2 tablespoons of sugar and $\frac{1}{4}$ teaspoon of cinnamon.

● Add the apple chunks and toss with the fork until
the pieces are evenly coated with the cinnamon-sugar.

● Pour the apple chunks into the prepared dish,
spreading them out evenly with the fork. Set aside.

4 Make the batter.

● In the blender, combine the remaining sugar, the
remaining cinnamon, the eggs, milk, flour, and vanilla.

● Put the lid on securely and, holding the lid down
tightly, blend on medium speed for about 1 minute,
until all the ingredients are well mixed and frothy.

eat the pancake while it's warm and puffy!

5 Bake the apples.

● Put the dish in the oven and bake the apple chunks for 5 minutes.

● Using an oven mitt, carefully pull out the oven rack until the dish is visible. Do not remove the dish.

● Pour the batter evenly over the apples. Slide the rack back into the oven and close the oven door.

6 Bake the pancake.

● Bake the pancake for about 25 minutes, until puffed and brown.

● Using oven mitts, carefully remove the dish from the oven and set it on the cooling rack.

● Dust the pancake with icing sugar using the fine-mesh sieve (see page 13). Cut into wedges and serve immediately.

buttermilk biscuits

makes **6** large biscuits

what you need!

 ingredients

plain flour 285 g (10 oz) , plus extra for work surface

sugar 3 tablespoons

baking powder 1 tablespoon

salt 3/4 teaspoon

very cold butter 85 g (3 oz), cut into chunks

buttermilk 240 ml (8 fl oz)

 tools

measuring cups, spoons, & scale

medium mixing bowl

wooden spoon

pastry blender or 2 table knives

7¹/₂-cm round biscuit cutter or cookie cutter

baking sheet

oven mitts

cooling rack

1 Mix the dry ingredients.

- Preheat the oven to 200°C.

- In the medium bowl, using the wooden spoon, stir together the flour, sugar, baking powder, and salt.

2 Make and shape the dough.

- Scatter the butter over the flour mixture. Cut the butter into the flour with the pastry blender or 2 table knives (see page 9). The mixture is ready when it looks like coarse crumbs with small pieces of butter still visible.

- Add the buttermilk and stir gently with the wooden spoon until the mixture starts to clump together.

- Sprinkle a work surface with some flour. Dump the shaggy dough onto it and gently press it into a rough, thick oval.

3 Cut out the biscuits and bake.

- Cut a round out of the dough with the biscuit cutter. Lift the cutter and set the biscuit on the baking sheet. Repeat, cutting as close as possible to the previous shape and spacing the biscuits about 5 cm apart on the baking sheet.

- Gather up the scraps, gently press together, and cut out more biscuits.

- Put the baking sheet in the oven and bake for 15 to 18 minutes, until the biscuits are puffed and brown. Using oven mitts, remove the baking sheet from the oven and set it on the cooling rack to cool for 10 minutes.

simple breads & muffins 95

easy!
popovers

makes **12** popovers

what you need!

ingredients

large eggs 4, at room temperature

whole milk 300 ml (10 fl oz) , at room temperature

vegetable oil 3 tablespoons

plain flour 140 g (5 oz)

salt $3/4$ teaspoon

butter or jam for serving (optional)

tools

measuring cups, spoons, & scale

12-cup nonstick muffin pan

electric blender

oven mitts

cooling rack

wooden skewer

1 Before you start.

- Preheat the oven to 220°C. Heavily grease the muffin pan cups with butter.

3 Fill the cups.

- Pour the batter into the prepared muffin cups, dividing it evenly and filling each cup about three-fourths full.

2 Make the batter.

- In the blender, combine the eggs, milk, and oil. Put the lid on securely and, holding the lid down tightly, blend on medium speed for about 10 seconds, until all the ingredients are combined.

- Turn off the blender, uncover, add the flour and salt, and re-cover. Again, hold the lid down tightly. Blend for 15 more seconds, until combined.

4 Bake and pierce the popovers.

- Put the pan in the oven and bake for about 28 minutes, until the popovers are puffed and well browned. Do not open the oven door while the popovers are baking or they may not rise correctly.

- Using oven mitts, remove the pan from the oven. Immediately tip the popovers out of the pan onto a work surface or the cooling rack.

- Pierce each popover with the wooden skewer to allow the steam to escape. Serve immediately with butter or jam (if using).

yeast breads

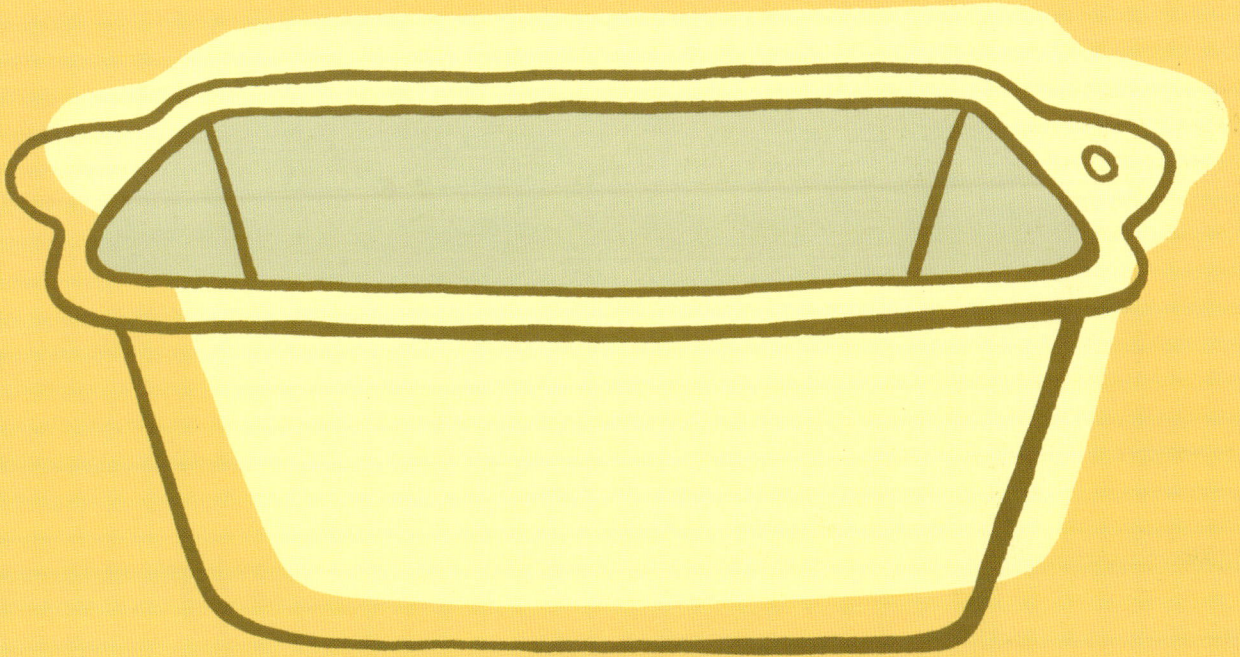

Did you know yeast is a living organism that eats sugar and breathes carbon dioxide?

white loaf bread

makes **1** loaf

Note: This recipe takes extra time, see steps 4 and 6.

This recipe takes extra time, see steps 4 and 6.

what you need!

ingredients

plain flour 425 g (15 oz), plus extra for kneading

rapid-rise yeast 7 g (¹/₄ oz)

sugar 2 tablespoons

salt 1 teaspoon

water 240 ml (8 fl oz)

butter 55 g (2 oz), cut into chunks

vegetable oil 3 teaspoons

tools

measuring cups, spoons, & scale

large mixing bowl

wooden spoon

medium saucepan

pot holder

instant-read thermometer

plastic wrap

21¹/₂-by-11¹/₂-cm metal loaf pan

ruler

pastry brush

oven mitts

cooling rack

1 Mix the dry ingredients.

● In the large bowl, using the wooden spoon, stir together the flour, yeast, sugar, and salt.

2 Make the dough.

● Heat the water and butter in the medium saucepan over medium heat, stirring with the wooden spoon until the butter melts. Move the pan to a heatproof surface using the pot holder.

● The liquid must be between 46° and 52°C. Use the instant-read thermometer to check the temperature.

● Pour the warm liquid into the flour mixture and stir with the wooden spoon until a rough, shaggy dough forms.

3 Knead the dough.

● Sprinkle a work surface with some flour. Dump the dough onto the surface. Knead the dough, flouring your hands and the surface with more flour as needed to prevent sticking.

● To knead, gather the dough together, then push the top part of the dough away from you with the heel of one hand. Fold that piece over the dough. Give the dough a quarter turn and repeat. Keep kneading for about 10 minutes, until the dough is smooth and no longer sticky.

4 Let the dough rise.

● Gather the dough into a ball. Wipe out the bowl and oil it with about 1 teaspoon of vegetable oil.

● Put the dough into the bowl and turn the ball to coat it with oil. Cover the bowl tightly with plastic wrap. Set the bowl in a warm spot and let the dough rise for about 45 minutes, until doubled in size. Poke the dough with your finger to see if it is ready (see page 116).

● Lightly oil the loaf pan with about 1 teaspoon of the vegetable oil.

● Dump out the risen dough, rounded side up, onto a clean work surface and press gently to deflate.

try a piece with **butter** or a spoonful of **jam!**

5 Shape the loaf.

● Gently shape the dough into a 20-by-30-cm rectangle.

● Beginning at one of the short sides, roll up the dough to form a loaf. Pinch the long seam and the ends together to seal. Press gently but firmly on the log until it forms a smooth, 20-by-10-cm rectangle with a slightly domed top.

● Place the dough, seam side down, into the prepared pan. Press on the dough to flatten slightly and fill the pan evenly.

6 Glaze the dough and let it rise.

● Use the pastry brush to brush the top of the dough with the remaining 1 teaspoon vegetable oil.

● Cover the pan loosely with a large piece of plastic wrap. Set the pan in a warm spot and let the dough rise for about 40 minutes, until doubled in size and the center is $2^1/2$ cm above the rim.

7 Bake and cool the bread.

● About 15 minutes before the dough is ready, preheat the oven to 220°C. When the dough is ready, remove the plastic wrap. Put the pan in the oven and bake the bread for about 35 minutes, until the top is brown.

● Using oven mitts, remove the pan from the oven. Turn the pan on its side on the cooling rack and slip the loaf out. Let cool completely on its side before slicing.

cinnamon-raisin swirl bread

makes **1** loaf

Note: This is an advanced recipe and takes extra time, see step 4.

ingredients

DOUGH

plain flour 425 g (15 oz), plus extra for kneading

rapid-rise yeast 7 g (¹/₄ oz)

sugar 2 tablespoons

salt 1 teaspoon

water 240 ml (8 fl oz)

butter 55 g (2 oz), cut into chunks

vegetable oil 3 teaspoons

FILLING

sultanas 125 g (4 oz)

sugar 60 g (2 oz)

ground cinnamon 1 tablespoon

tools

measuring cups, spoons, & scale

large & small mixing bowls

wooden spoon

small saucepan

pot holder

instant-read thermometer

plastic wrap

21¹/₂-by-11¹/₂-cm metal loaf pan

ruler

pastry brush

oven mitts

cooling rack

1 Prepare the dough and filling.

• Using the dough ingredients listed here, prepare the White Loaf Bread recipe through step 4 (pages 101 to 102).

• In the small bowl, using the wooden spoon, stir together the sultanas, sugar, and cinnamon to make the filling.

2 Fill the dough.

• On a clean work surface, gently shape the dough into a 20-by-30-cm rectangle.

• Pour the cinnamon-raisin mixture out onto the dough. Spread it out evenly over the dough, leaving a border around the edge, and press in lightly with your fingers.

3 Shape the loaf.

• Beginning at one of the short sides, roll up the dough to form a loaf.

• Pinch the long seam and the ends together to seal in the cinnamon-raisin mixture. Press gently but firmly on the log until it forms a smooth, 20-by-10-cm rectangle with a slightly domed top.

• Place the dough, seam side down, into the prepared pan. Press on the dough to flatten slightly and fill the pan evenly.

4 Finish and bake the bread.

• Brush the top of the dough with the remaining 1 teaspoon vegetable oil. Cover the pan loosely with a large piece of plastic wrap. Set the pan in a warm spot and let the dough rise for about 40 minutes, until doubled in size and the center is 2 1/2 cm above the rim.

• About 15 minutes before the dough is ready, preheat the oven to 220°C. When the dough is ready, remove the plastic wrap. Put the pan in the oven and bake the bread for about 35 minutes, until the top is brown.

• Using oven mitts, remove the pan from the oven. Turn the pan on its side on the cooling rack and slip the loaf out. Let cool completely on its side before slicing.

pretzels

makes **10** large pretzels

Note: This is an advanced recipe and takes extra time, see step 3.

plain flour 425 g (15 oz), plus extra for kneading

rapid-rise yeast 7 g (¼ oz)

sugar 1 tablespoon

salt 1 teaspoon

warm water 240 ml (8 fl oz)

vegetable oil 3 tablespoons plus 3 teaspoons

bicarbonate of soda 2 tablespoons

coarse salt 2 tablespoons

tools

measuring cups, spoons, & scale

large & small mixing bowls

wooden spoon

instant-read thermometer

plastic wrap

2 baking sheets

sharp knife

ruler

large stainless-steel saucepan

large heatproof slotted spoon

oven mitts

cooling racks

1 Prepare the dough.

● In the large bowl, using the wooden spoon, stir together the flour, yeast, sugar, and salt.

● The warm water must be between 46° and 52°C. Use the instant-read thermometer to check the temperature. Pour the water and the 3 tablespoons vegetable oil into the flour mixture. Stir with the wooden spoon until a rough, shaggy dough forms.

2 Knead the dough.

● Sprinkle a work surface with some flour. Dump the dough onto the surface.

● Knead the dough for about 10 minutes, until it is smooth and no longer sticky (see page 102). Flour your hands and the surface with more flour as needed to prevent sticking.

3 Let the dough rise.

● Gather the dough into a ball. Wipe out the bowl and oil it with about 1 teaspoon of vegetable oil.

● Put the dough into the bowl and turn the ball to coat it with oil. Cover the bowl tightly with plastic wrap. Set the bowl in a warm spot and let the dough rise for about 45 minutes, until doubled in size. Poke the dough with your finger to see if it is ready (see page 116).

4 Form the ropes.

● Oil 2 baking sheets with the remaining 2 teaspoons oil.

● Dump out the risen dough onto a clean work surface and press gently to deflate. Cut the dough into 10 equal pieces with the knife.

● Work with 1 piece of dough at a time and keep the remaining pieces loosely covered with plastic wrap. Using the palms of your hands, roll the dough into a rope about 50 cm long, adding flour only if needed to prevent sticking. Repeat with the remaining dough pieces.

5 Twist the ropes.

● Twist each rope into a pretzel by making an oval about $7^{1}/_{2}$ cm wide. At the top of the oval, twist the rope together twice.

6 Form the pretzels.

● Bring the ends of the rope to the bottom of the oval so that the twist is in the middle. Press down the ends so the dough sticks.

● Divide the pretzels evenly between the 2 prepared baking sheets. Cover the pretzels loosely with plastic wrap. Set the baking sheet in a warm spot and let the pretzels rise for about 20 minutes, until puffed and doubled in size.

● While the pretzels are rising, preheat the oven to 230°C.

be extra **careful** when boiling the pretzels!

7 Boil the pretzels.

● Fill the large saucepan two-thirds full of water and stir in the bicarbonate of soda with the slotted spoon. Bring the water to a rolling boil over high heat.

● Remove the plastic wrap from the pretzels. Ask an adult to help you boil the pretzels. Using the slotted spoon, lift a pretzel from the baking sheet and carefully slip it into the boiling water. Be careful: the water and steam are very hot!

● Boil the pretzel for about 30 seconds, until it floats to the surface. Turn the pretzel over with the spoon and boil for 30 more seconds.

● Using the slotted spoon, remove the pretzel and return it to the baking sheet. Repeat with the remaining pretzels, placing them about 5 cm apart.

8 Salt and bake the pretzels.

● Sprinkle each pretzel with a big pinch of coarse salt.

● Put 1 baking sheet in the oven and bake the pretzels for about 15 minutes, until they are deep golden brown. Using oven mitts, remove the baking sheet from the oven and set it on the cooling rack to cool completely. Repeat with the remaining pretzels.

what you need!

ingredients

DOUGH

plain flour 425 g (15 oz), plus extra for kneading

rapid-rise yeast 7 g (¼ oz)

sugar 1 teaspoon

salt 2 teaspoons

warm water 240 ml (8 fl oz)

olive oil 3 tablespoons

vegetable oil 3 teaspoons

TOPPING

garlic 1 small clove

fresh herbs 2 teaspoons chopped; choose from rosemary, oregano, thyme, or a mixture (optional)

coarse salt 1 teaspoon

olive oil 4 tablespoons

tools

measuring cups, spoons, & scale

large & small mixing bowls

wooden spoon

instant-read thermometer

plastic wrap

large baking sheet with 2½-cm sides

cutting board

metal spatula

large, sharp knife

table fork

oven mitts

cooling racks

focaccia

makes **1** large focaccia

Note: This recipe takes extra time, see step 3.

1 Make the dough.

● In the large bowl, using the wooden spoon, stir together the flour, yeast, sugar, and salt.

● The warm water must be between 46° and 52°C. Use the instant-read thermometer to check the temperature. Pour the water and olive oil into the flour mixture. Stir with the wooden spoon until a rough, shaggy dough forms.

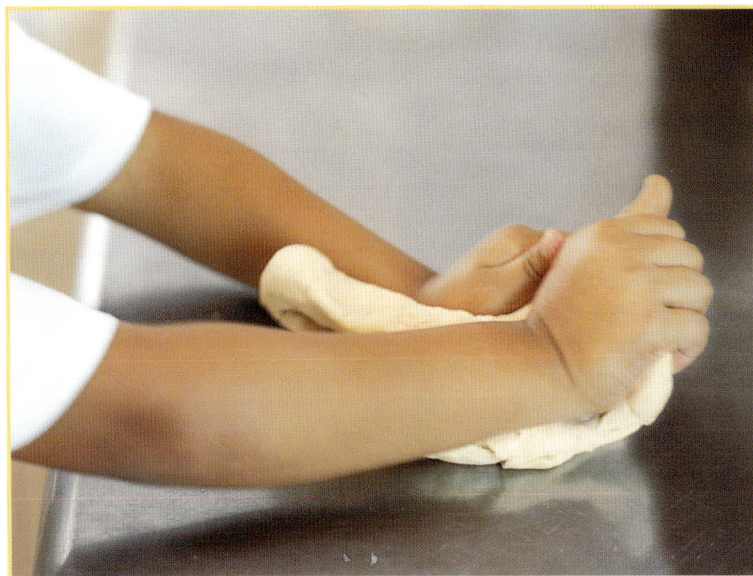

2 Knead the dough.

● Dump the dough onto a work surface.

● Knead the dough for about 10 minutes, until it is smooth and no longer sticky (see page 102). Flour your hands and the surface only if needed to prevent sticking.

3 Let the dough rise.

● Gather the dough into a ball. Wipe out the bowl and oil it with about 1 teaspoon of vegetable oil.

● Put the dough into the bowl and turn the ball to coat it with oil. Cover the bowl tightly with plastic wrap. Set the bowl in a warm spot and let the dough rise until doubled in size, about 45 minutes. Poke the dough with your finger to see if it is ready (see page 116).

4 Shape the dough.

● Oil the baking sheet with 1 teaspoon of the vegetable oil. Remove the dough from the bowl, place it on the prepared baking sheet, and press gently to deflate.

● Using your hands, gently stretch the dough into a 25-by-18-cm oval.

● Brush the dough with the remaining 1 teaspoon vegetable oil and cover loosely with a large piece of plastic wrap.

● Set the pan in a warm spot and let the dough rise for about 20 minutes, until puffed and doubled in size.

make a foccacia sandwich with this bread!

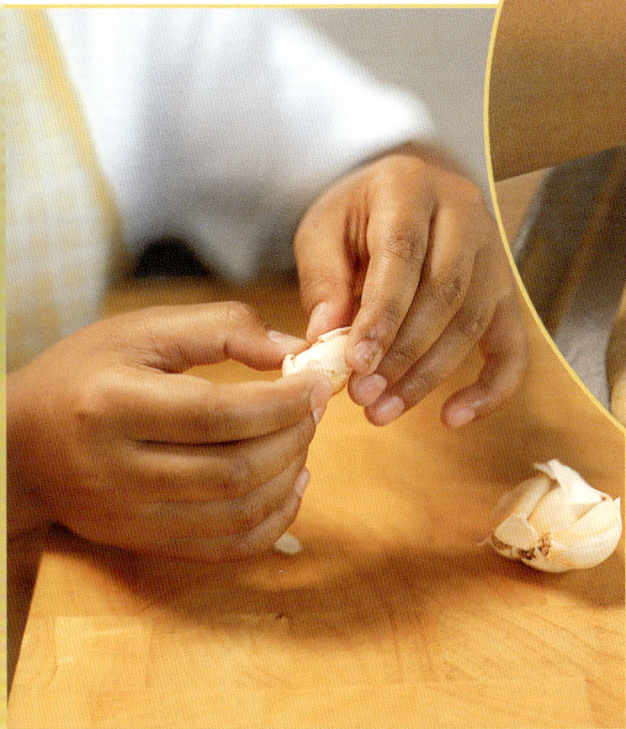

5 Prepare the topping.

● Preheat the oven to 220°C.

● Smash the garlic clove on the cutting board with the metal spatula. Peel away the skin.

● Chop the garlic into small pieces with the large, sharp knife. In the small bowl, stir together the garlic, herbs (if using), and coarse salt with the fork.

6 Finish and bake the focaccia.

● When the dough is ready, remove the plastic wrap. Press the tips of your fingers into the dough all over the surface to create "dimples."

● Scatter the garlic mixture evenly over the dough. Drizzle the top of the dough evenly with 2 tablespoons of the olive oil.

● Put the pan in the oven and bake the focaccia for 25 to 30 minutes, until puffed and the top is browned.

● Using oven mitts, remove the baking sheet from the oven and set it on the cooling rack. Drizzle the focaccia evenly with the remaining 2 tablespoons olive oil. Let cool for 15 minutes before serving.

what you need!

ingredients

DOUGH

plain flour 355 g (12¹/₂ oz), plus extra for kneading

rapid-rise yeast 7 g (¹/₄ oz)

sugar 2 teaspoons

salt 2¹/₂ teaspoons

warm water 240 ml (8 fl oz)

olive oil 2 tablespoons

vegetable oil 1 teaspoon

TOPPING

mozzarella cheese 170 g (6 oz)

tomato or spaghetti sauce 250 ml (8 fl oz)

pepperoni 25 slices (optional)

tools

measuring cups, spoons, & scale

large & small mixing bowls

wooden spoon

instant-read thermometer

plastic wrap

large baking sheet with 2¹/₂-cm sides

baking paper

box grater-shredder

ruler

large spoon

oven mitts

cutting board

pizza wheel

pizza

makes **1** large pizza

Note: This recipe takes extra time, see step 3.

1 Make the dough.

● In the large bowl, using the wooden spoon, stir together the flour, yeast, sugar, and salt.

● The warm water must be between 46° and 52°C. Use the instant-read thermometer to check the temperature. Pour the water and olive oil into the flour mixture. Stir with the wooden spoon until a rough, shaggy dough forms.

2 Knead the dough.

● Sprinkle a work surface with some flour. Dump the dough onto the surface.

● Knead the dough for about 10 minutes, until it is smooth and no longer sticky (see page 102). Flour your hands and the surface with more flour as needed to prevent sticking.

3 Let the dough rise.

● Gather the dough into a ball. Wipe out the bowl and oil it with about 1 teaspoon of vegetable oil.

● Put the dough into the bowl, and turn the ball to coat the surface with oil. Cover the bowl tightly with plastic wrap. Set the bowl in a warm spot and let the dough rise for about 45 minutes, until doubled in size.

● To see if the dough is ready, poke it with your finger. If the indent from your finger stays, the dough is ready. If it bounces back, let the dough sit for 10 more minutes.

4 Shred the cheese.

● Hold the box grater-shredder firmly on a work surface with 1 hand. Use your other hand to slide the chunk of mozzarella cheese over the large holes to create shreds. Keep your fingers safely away from the holes.

5 Shape the dough.

● Put the oven rack in the lowest position. Preheat the oven to 230°C. Line the baking sheet with baking paper.

● Sprinkle the work surface with some flour. Dump out the risen dough and press gently to deflate.

● Using your hands, gently stretch the dough into a 35-cm round. Slide your hands under the dough and carefully lift it onto the prepared baking sheet.

leave off the
pepperoni and make a
gooey cheese
pizza!

6 Add the sauce.

● Pour the sauce onto the dough and spread it out evenly with the back of the large spoon. Leave a 2¹/₂-cm border of dough around the edge.

7 Finish and bake the pizza.

● Sprinkle the cheese over the sauce, and arrange the pepperoni slices (if using) on top.

● Put the baking sheet on the bottom rack in the oven and bake the pizza for about 15 minutes, until the cheese is bubbling and the crust is brown.

● Using oven mitts, remove the baking sheet from the oven and slide the pizza onto the cutting board. Using the pizza wheel, cut into wedges. Serve immediately.

ingredients

DOUGH

plain flour 495 g (17^1/$_2$ oz), plus extra for kneading

rapid-rise yeast 7 g (^{1}/$_4$ oz)

sugar 60 g (2 oz)

salt ^{3}/$_4$ teaspoon

whole milk 240 ml (8 fl oz)

butter 100 g (3 ^{3}/$_4$ oz), cut into chunks

large egg 1

vegetable oil 2 teaspoons

TOPPING

large egg 1

water 1 tablespoon

poppy seeds or sesame seeds 1 tablespoon

tools

measuring cups, spoons, & scale

large & small mixing bowls

wooden spoon

small saucepan

pot holder

instant-read thermometer

plastic wrap

sharp knife

ruler

baking sheet

table fork

pastry brush

oven mitts

cooling rack

braided egg bread

makes **1** loaf

Note: This is an advanced recipe and takes extra time, see steps 3 and 5.

1 Make the dough.

● In the large bowl, using the wooden spoon, stir together the flour, yeast, sugar, and salt.

● Heat the milk and butter in the small saucepan over medium heat, stirring with the wooden spoon until the butter melts. Move the pan to a heatproof surface with the pot holder.

● The liquid must be between 46° and 52°C. Use the instant-read thermometer to check the temperature.

● Pour the warm liquid into the flour mixture. Add the egg and stir with the wooden spoon until a rough, shaggy dough forms.

2 Knead the dough.

● Sprinkle a work surface with some flour. Dump the dough onto the surface.

● Knead the dough for about 10 minutes, until it is smooth and no longer sticky (see page 102). Flour your hands and the surface with more flour as needed to prevent sticking.

make this bread for a special occasion!

3 Let the dough rise.

● Gather the dough into a ball. Wipe out the bowl and oil it with about 1 teaspoon of vegetable oil.

● Put the dough into the bowl and turn the ball to coat it with oil. Cover the bowl tightly with plastic wrap. Set the bowl in a warm spot and let the dough rise for about 45 minutes, until doubled in size. Poke the dough with your finger to see if it is ready (see page 116).

● Dump out the risen dough onto a clean work surface and press gently to deflate.

4 Form the ropes.

● Cut the dough into 3 equal pieces with the sharp knife.

● Work with 1 piece of dough at a time and keep the remaining pieces loosely covered with plastic wrap. Using the palms of your hands, roll the dough into a rope about 50 cm long, adding flour only if needed to prevent sticking. Repeat with the remaining 2 pieces.

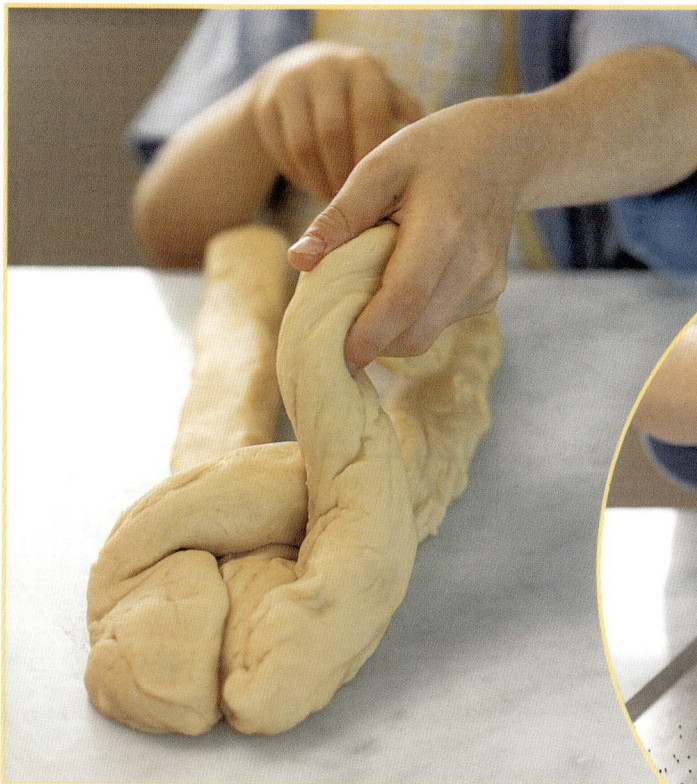

5 Braid the dough.

- Arrange the 3 ropes side by side and pinch the tops together. Starting at the top, braid the ropes by alternating the far left rope over the middle rope and then the far right rope over the middle rope until you reach the end.

- Pinch the bottom ends of the ropes together and tuck them under the loaf.

- Oil the baking sheet with the remaining 1 teaspoon oil.

- Move the braid to the prepared baking sheet. Cover the braid loosely with plastic wrap. Set the baking sheet in a warm spot and let the braid rise for about 30 minutes, until puffed and doubled in size.

6 Decorate and bake the bread.

- About 15 minutes before the dough is ready, preheat the oven to 200°C. In the small bowl, beat together the egg and water with the fork.

- When the dough is ready, remove the plastic wrap. Use the pastry brush to gently brush the braid with the egg mixture. Sprinkle the braid with the seeds.

- Put the pan in the oven and bake the bread for about 28 minutes, until it is brown. Using oven mitts, remove the baking sheet from the oven and set it on the cooling rack to cool completely.

glossary

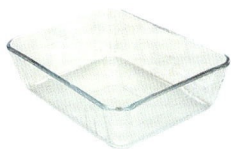

baking dish

baking sheet

box grater-shredder

cake pan

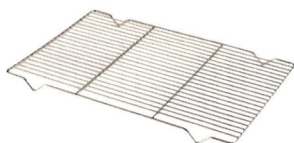

cooling rack

electric mixer

icing spatula

instant-read
thermometer

loaf pan

muffin pan

baking paper

pastry blender

pastry brushes

pie dish

rolling pin

rubber spatula

sieve

sifter

springform pan

vegetable peeler

This alphabetical list explains many of the words and ingredients you'll find in this cookbook.

b

bake
To cook with hot, dry air in an oven.

baking powder
A white chemical powder made by combining bicarbonate of soda, an acid such as cream of tartar, and cornflour. Makes some doughs and batters rise during baking.

bicarbonate of soda
A white chemical powder that, when combined with an acid ingredient such as sour cream or buttermilk, releases carbon dioxide gas, causing a batter to rise in the oven.

beat
To mix ingredients vigorously, stirring with a spoon, fork, or beaters in a circular motion.

blend
To combine two or more ingredients thoroughly. Also, to mix ingredients in an electric blender.

boil
To heat a liquid until bubbles constantly rise to its surface and break. A gentle boil is when small bubbles rise and break slowly. A rolling boil is when large bubbles rise and break quickly.

buttermilk
A type of milk that has "cultures" added to it and is similar to yogurt. It is often used in desserts and baked goods, and has a tangy flavor and thick texture.

c

chocolate
Chocolate is available in many different forms, including plain chocolate, a dark, sweet chocolate sold in blocks, bars, and chips; and unsweetened chocolate, a bitter product with a strong chocolate flavor sold in small squares or blocks. Unsweetened cocoa powder is a fine, bitter powder with a strong chocolate flavor; it is different from hot cocoa mix because it includes no sugar or milk products.

chop
To cut food into pieces using a sharp knife. Finely chopped pieces are small; coarsely chopped pieces are large.

cinnamon
A light brown powder that is made by grinding the bark of a tropical evergreen tree. Cinnamon has a mildly sweet flavor and is widely used in baking.

coconut, shredded
The shredded and dried snowy white meat of the world's largest nut. Available sweetened or unsweetened in bags or cans.

cornflour
A very fine powder made by grinding the center (known as the endosperm) of corn kernels. Used as a thickener.

corn syrup
A thick, sweet syrup made from corn; available in two types, light and dark. Used mostly in icings to prevent sugar from forming crystals and making the icing lumpy.

cream cheese
A soft, spreadable cheese with a mildly tangy flavor; made from cow's milk.

cream, double
Also called whipping cream, double cream has a thick, rich consistency because it contains a high percentage of milk fat.

crush
To press down on an ingredient, such as a graham cracker or hard candy, with a tool (like a rolling pin) or your hands to make the ingredient into crumbs.

d

disk
Dough that has been formed into a flat, round shape.

dissolve
To mix a fine-textured, solid substance, such as sugar or salt, with a liquid until the solid disappears.

divide
To split a batch of dough, batter, or ingredients into smaller, equal batches.

drizzle
To pour a liquid, such as oil, back and forth lightly over food in a thin stream.

dust
To cover a food, your hands, or a work surface lightly with flour or sugar.

e

eggs
Sold in a range of sizes. Use eggs marked "large" for the recipes in this book.

f

flour, plain
The most common flour available, composed of a blend of wheats so that it works equally well for cakes, cookies, and other baked goods.

g

galette
A French country tart that is made with pie dough and is usually filled with fresh fruit. Unlike most pies and tarts, it is often baked without a pie or tart pan, usually on a baking sheet.

graham cracker
A wholemeal, honey-sweetened rectangular cookie often used as crumbs.

grate
To slide an ingredient, such carrots, across a surface of small, sharp-edged holes on a box grater-shredder to create tiny pieces.

grease
To rub a baking pan or dish evenly with butter or oil to prevent sticking.

h

heatproof
Dishes or surfaces that can come in contact with high heat without damaging them.

i

invert
To turn a piece of cookware, usually a pan containing a cake, upside down so that the food falls gently onto a cooling rack or a plate.

k

knead
To work dough with your hands, using pressing, folding, and turning motions. When dough is fully kneaded, it is smooth and no longer sticky.

l

lattice
Strips of dough overlapping in a crisscross pattern, usually over a pie filling.

lengthwise
In the same direction as, or parallel to, the longest side of a piece of food or a pan.

line
To cover the bottom of a cake pan, baking sheet or other pan with a piece of baking paper or aluminum foil to prevent sticking.

m

melt
To heat a solid substance, such as butter or chocolate, until it becomes liquid.

mix
To stir together dry or wet ingredients until combined.

molasses
A thick, sticky syrup made from raw sugar and ranging from light to dark brown.

mound
To heap into a raised mass.

n

nutmeg
A fragrant spice ground from the seed of a tropical tree.

o

oil, olive
Flavorful cooking oil pressed from olives.

oil, vegetable
Bland-tasting cooking oil made by blending corn, safflower, and/or other vegetable-based oils.

p

peak
Whipped cream or egg whites can be whipped to form peaks. Medium-firm peaks should be soft but firm enough to hold their shape, and form a curl at the top of the beater when lifted.

peel
To strip or cut away the skin or rind from fruits and vegetables.

popover
A light, hollow muffinlike bread made with eggs, milk, and flour.

preheat
To heat an oven to a specific temperature before use.

puff pastry
A light, flaky pastry formed by rolling and folding butter and dough into hundreds of thin layers that expand when the pastry is baked.

r

refrigerate
To place food in the refrigerator to chill or to become firm.

rise
What happens to a dough or batter when it becomes bigger as a result of the gas released by the yeast, baking powder, or bicarbonate of soda that the dough contains.

roll out
To flatten dough with a rolling pin until it is smooth, even, and usually thin.

room temperature
The temperature of a comfortable room. Butter is often brought to room temperature so it will soften and blend easily.

s

salt
Salt brings out the flavors of food, even sweet baked

goods! It can be fine-grained, like regular salt, or coarse.

seeds, poppy
Black, tiny, round seeds used as a topping or a filling for breads and pastries.

seeds, sesame
Pale, tan, small, flat seeds used as topping for breads and pastries.

set
When a filling or a liquid becomes more solid, such as when a cheesecake finishes baking, the center is "set."

set aside
To put ingredients to one side while you do something else.

shred
To cut an ingredient on the medium or large holes of a box grater-shredder.

sift
To put an ingredient, such as flour or sugar, through a sifter or a fine-mesh sieve to get rid of any lumps or coarse particles.

simmer
To heat a liquid to just below boiling. The surface of the liquid should be steaming.

slice
To cut food lengthwise or crosswise with a knife, forming thick or thin pieces.

sour cream
A tangy, smooth cream made by making fresh cream sour.

spread
To apply a soft mixture or ingredient, such as frosting or butter, over another food in an even layer.

stir
To move a spoon, fork, whisk, or other utensil continuously through dry or wet ingredients, usually in a circular pattern.

sugar
The three most common sugars are granulated sugar, small, white granules that pour easily; icing sugar, which is granulated sugar finely ground and mixed with a small amount of cornflour; and brown sugar, a moist blend of granulated sugar and molasses. Brown sugar is sold in two basic types: light (also known as golden) and dark. When a recipe calls for "sugar," always use granulated sugar.

sultanas
A dried sweet grape. Sultanas come in two basic types, dark and golden.

sweetened condensed milk
Milk that has most of the water removed from it and is mixed with sugar. It is thick, creamy, and very sweet and you buy it in a can. This is not the same as evaporated milk.

t

thicken
When a food changes from a loose, liquid consistency to a thick, firmer one.

toss
To mix ingredients, such as butter and flour, by tumbling them together with both of your hands, two forks, or two spoons.

trim
To cut food so that it is uniform in size and shape. Also, to cut away any unneeded or inedible part.

v

vanilla essence
A liquid flavoring made from vanilla beans, the dried pods of a type of orchid.

W

whisk
Describes the tool and the action. A whisk is made of loops of sturdy wire that are attached to a handle. To whisk something means to stir a liquid such as cream or egg whites vigorously with a whisk, adding air and thereby increasing its volume.

work surface
A flat space, such as a kitchen counter or a kitchen work table, used for cutting, mixing, or preparing foods.

y

yeast, rapid-rise
Microscopic plants known as yeasts make breads rise. In recent years, rapid-rise yeast has been developed to make breads rise in only half the usual time.

yogurt
A custardlike dairy food with a tart flavor, prepared from milk. Plain yogurt, often used in baking, is unsweetened and unflavored.

z

zest
The thin, brightly colored outer layer of peel of a citrus fruit. It is most often grated or cut into pieces.

index

This edition published for INDEX BOOKS Ltd 2005

WILLIAMS-SONOMA, INC.
Founder & Vice-Chairman: Chuck Williams

WELDON OWEN INC.
Chief Executive Officer: John Owen
President: Terry Newell
Chief Operating Officer: Larry Partington
Vice President International Sales: Stuart Laurence
Creative Director: Gaye Allen
Associate Creative Director: Leslie Harrington
Publisher: Hannah Rahill
Series Editor: Kim Goodfriend
Editor: Tanya Henry
Copy Editor: Sharon Silva
Assistant Editor: Donita Boles
Art Director: Teri Gardiner
Designer: Teri Gardiner
Production Director: Chris Hemesath
Color Specialist: Teri Bell and Kathy Schermerhorn
Production and Reprint Coordinator: Todd Rechner
Proofreader: Kris Balloun
Indexer: Ken DellaPenta
Food Stylists: Lori De Mori and Tara Brogan
Consulting Editor: Lisa Atwood
Educational Consultant: Diana Motsinger

Weldon Owen would like to thank Sheri Giblin for additional photography (pages 30, 49, 77, 85, and 106). Many thanks to all of our wonderful testers (and samplers, too!): Alex and Tierney Dodge, Alexa and Lee Tilghman, Abigail Lupoff, Bonnie and Emily Lee, Caroline Clark, Eliza Murphy, Kelley and Jamie Hodge, Libby Welke, Nick and Ellie Smith. We would also like to thank our wonderful kid models: Maddison and Holly Brogan, Caterina Detti, Freddy Riddiford, Sasha McEwen, Sam and Eliza Beca, Jammel Liuaga, and Robert Wong. A special thanks to Ursula Bena, who made all of the beautiful aprons and an extra special thanks to the lovely Brogan family for their model search and scheduling prowess and their magnificent house and hospitality.

Conceived and produced by
WELDON OWEN INC.
814 Montgomery Street, San Francisco, CA 94133
Telephone 415-291-0100 Fax 415-291-8841

In Collaboration with Williams-Sonoma Inc.
3250 Van Ness Avenue, San Francisco, CA 94109

A WELDON OWEN PRODUCTION
Copyright © 2003 Weldon Owen Inc. and Williams-Sonoma Inc.

This edition first printed in 2005
10 9 8 7 6 5 4 3 2 1

ISBN 1-89237-445-5

Printed in China by Midas Printing Limited

abigail johnson dodge

is a Paris-trained author, culinary instructor, and pastry chef. She has been an editor at *Woman's Day* and *Parents* magazines, and currently directs the test kitchen for *Fine Cooking* magazine. Dodge is the author of the Williams-Sonoma *Kid's Cookbook, Great Fruit Desserts,* was a contributor to *Cookies for Christmas* and the *All New All-Purpose Joy of Cooking,* and created Cooking in the Classroom, an elementary school program that teaches kids how to cook. Her own young son and daughter, Alex and Tierney, are enthusiastic cooks and tasters, especially if the samples are chocolate.

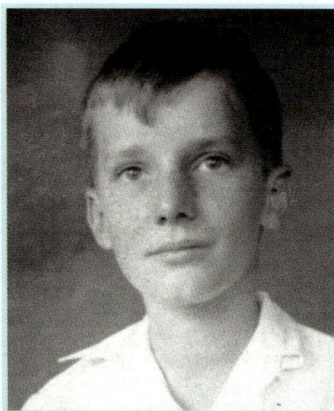

Abby at age 10

chuck williams

has helped to revolutionize cooking in America. He opened his first Williams-Sonoma store in the California wine country town of Sonoma in 1956, later moving it to San Francisco. More than two hundred stores are now open in the United States, and the company's catalog has an annual circulation of more than 40 million. The philosophy behind his success is aptly summed up by the title of the cookbook he wrote to chronicle William-Sonoma's first 40 years: *Celebrating the Pleasures of Cooking.*

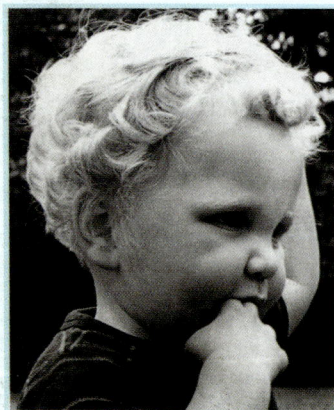

Chuck at age 12

jason lowe

is an award-winning photographer specializing in food and travel. Lowe's work has appeared in numerous magazines and cookbooks, including *Savoring Tuscany* and *Savoring Provence* in the Williams-Sonoma *Savoring* ® series and Williams-Sonoma *Essentials of Grilling.* Lowe lives in London, England.

Jason at age 2